FIRST CATCH YOUR CALAMARI

FIRST CATCH YOUR CALAMARI

TRAVELS WITH AN APPETITE

A WRITER'S FOOD DIARY

JULIAN ROUP

Paperback ISBN 978-1-913762-97-1

This edition published in 2022 by BLKDOG Publishing.

A catalogue record for this book is available from the British Library.

www.blkdogpublishing.com

Other titles by Julian Roup for your consideration:

Life in a Time of Plague:

A Coronavirus Lockdown Diary

Into the Secret Heart of Ashdown Forest:

A Horseman's Country Diary

A Fisherman in the Saddle

For Jay and Jan who asked me for this book,
they are its salt and pepper.

François de la Rochefoucauld

'To eat is a necessity, but to eat intelligently is an art.'

Virginia Woolf

'One cannot think well, love well, sleep well, if not has not dined well.'

Irish Proverb

'Laughter is brightest where food is best.'

INTRODUCTION

To have grown up in Africa, white and well fed; and to write about food presents moral problems. My childhood and youth were spent in a food paradise, a cornucopia where many starved and some died of hunger. As I became increasingly aware of the injustices of South Africa's reality in the '60s and '70s, it was borne in on me that food was political.

My father owned a bakery. The price of bread was government controlled to keep this food staple at an affordable level, a small gesture from a brutal regime that served to heighten my political awareness of the role played by food in life, love and the pursuit of happiness, not to mention justice. This perspective has coloured my appreciation of food. It provides a view that looks askance at over-indulgence and the sometimes over-the-top offerings of some five star restaurants. And also, finally, a deep understanding that however sublime a sauce, or a dish, hunger remains the best sauce, appetite a very necessary implement to bring to the table for true enjoyment of a meal.

Food is political, it is a cultural vehicle, it is an expression of love and care and it is in its essence spiritual, in that it is essential to sustain life. Saying grace over a meal is a recognition of these things as much as the prayer said over an animal you have just killed. Food is life, so to have loved food is surely an indication of having loved life.

I was triply blessed growing up, as the son of a baker and the inheritor of two great food traditions, Jewish and Afrikaans. It was the basis for what I hope is an educated palate and an undiminished passion for eating well.

The Art of Cooking

I would argue that cooking is an art. And as such it is unique, for no other art requires the death of some of its elements, nor is any other art such a mix of the sacred and profane. To make it work, to feed people, ensuring their lives, some other creature must die, unless you are a vegetarian. This is not something that painting, writing, sculpture or music has to deal with.

Cooking spans a very wide range, from the creative and life-giving to its opposite. For many, it is an act of love repeated daily. And it is only now, in the last century, that cooks and chefs are achieving the kind of renown that artists have had for centuries. The humblest kitchen has something of the temple about it and the cook is a priest of sorts. There is much of ritual about cooking. The humblest sandwich, if made with love, is more than the sum of its parts.

Every religion incorporates food in its rituals, Christ's body and blood, the Easter Pascal Lamb, the Jews' unleavened bread, the abstinence from pork observed by both Muslims and Jews. Food carries with it a freight of meaning beyond taste. To eat well is one requirement of the good life, and not the least of it.

Our first act as humans is to take in our mother's milk. Food and the making and eating of it informs our cultures at many levels in complex ways and yet because we do it three times a day (if we are lucky) it remains a largely mundane activity, its meanings and values lost beneath the weight of growing it, shopping for it, preparing it and cleaning up after it's done.

When the Covid pandemic struck, we did not rush to church or hospital, we all rushed for food and toilet paper.

For me, cooking is informed by my love of good food; greed, if you will. It is for me a big part of the pleasure of being alive. Visiting a great food market beats every other kind of shopping. I find it exciting and intoxicating. To find myself of an evening in the kitchen after even the most tiring day is to experience a slowing down and a quietness that comes before the pleasure of eating. The act of cooking brings peace with it. It wasn't always so, there were nerves and spoiled food along the way, but these were milestones to the place I now find myself. Once the ingredients are selected, I don't have to think much about what needs to be done. I don't have to think of quantities or timing, the orchestration required by cooking looks after itself and I can simply enjoy the process.

The pleasure of cooking is enhanced by music or storytelling in the background. It also offers you the pleasure of good tools – a number of strong sharp knives for cutting vegetables and meat, a good garlic press, a selection of cast iron pots and pans, and a ridged grilling pan. Then there are the pleasures of scent as the cooking progresses, hot butter and garlic speak of serious intent and good things to come. The smell of baking bread and baked potatoes. The aromas of a great soup. Preparing the table with good crockery and cutlery and flowers, maybe candles. And these days of camera phones, the obligatory photo of the finished plate of food if you are pleased with it. And finally, the pleasure of those you've cooked for as the meal is enjoyed.

Much depends on what is currently available at home. I try to buy local and seasonal produce but thanks to the incredible international supply chain we eat things in mid-winter that our ancestors can only marvel at. A recent winter meal included asparagus from Chile, cherries from South Africa and butter from New Zealand. I know this is wrong and that the air-miles involved is not helping to save the earth, but I am fallible, and greed gets the better of me now and then.

For me the pleasures of food involve the shopping for it, the preparation, placing it on the table before my wife and family or friends and finally eating it. How many activities provide us with four distinct phases of pleasure? Not many.

One aspect of cooking culture that I so admire is the peasant ingenuity that informs the cooking of France and Italy and many other nations. The use of simple humble ingredients to produce something sublime with potatoes, rice, beans, onions, or the scrapings of the larder. Pasta, pizza, and so much of the best of Italy comes out of the need to make do with limited ingredients and no money for anything fancy. If you look to peasant cooking, you can eat sublimely well for very little outlay. A bean stew, a noodle and vegetable dish, an onion soup, frittata – the list is endless.

In all these things, flavour is king. If one has sun-ripened ingredients and the time to cook slowly, the robust flavours achieved can top many more elaborate dishes. And for me, if one has good fresh bread, sourdough by choice, and a glass of red wine, however humble, to accompany it, one has a meal that will satisfy the stomach as well as the soul.

Now and then I will toss the dice, throw caution to the wind and experiment. It does not always work out, but quite often it does, and then there is a new pleasure to be savoured. Sometimes it's the addition of something unusual to an old favourite – prunes to a beef stew; aniseed to a fish dish; frying a lettuce lightly in butter; or a goat's cheese baked with peppers. And so one's repertoire is widened, and new pleasures savoured.

But the world is changing, as it always does, and home cooking is a dying art in the West. I am astonished when I speak to younger neighbours who think nothing of ordering in a meal, delivered to their door, pizza, Indian, Chinese or a variety of other options including fish and chips. I wonder if they have any idea of the pleasures they are denying themselves, the joy of cooking?

To be fair, it must be a boon for young parents who both work and are dealing with children to simply lift the phone for a meal, but it is not cheap, and the ingredients are not always the best. And for the children, there is the danger of addiction to fast food.

One of the greatest gifts a parent can give a child is an educated palate, and an understanding of ingredients and cooking. This gift will enrich their lives and the lives of their own children in time. If we lose the will to cook, the world will have lost an art form, one that has defined us as a species from time immemorial. Let us continue to cook!

CHAPTER ONE

SALT RIVER MARKET - CAPE TOWN 1950S

This is not a book for foodies alone, this is a book for the hungry and for those who travel with an appetite. Some of my most memorable meals have not been in celebrated restaurants but those that live on in the good food cupboard of my mind, many of them taken with my feet in sea sand or lying in a field in France, or even in the army during my year of National Service and subsequent army camps. Believe it or not.

It is perhaps not surprising that I am passionate about food; my food heritage is broad. It comes out of the cuisine of Eastern European Jewry on my father's side and Dutch and French Huguenot settlers in South Africa on my mother's side. I was given two cultures and three languages: English, Afrikaans and some Yiddish, with a sprinkling of African language terms thrown in by way of spice.

One of my earliest food memories, and how appropriate for a future food lover, is of a visit with my mother to the Salt River food market in Cape Town in the mid-1950s. This was a veritable food circus. The place was a treasure house of the best that the Cape provided.

Little did I realise it then, at the age of five, that my

own family's DNA had been entwined with the Cape for more than 300 years. In 1660, my Dutch ancestor, Jan Pieterszoon an Caspel ter Mare (the surname Louw was added in 1689), arrived on the good ship *'t Ronde Bosje* at the Cape of Good Hope, also known for good reason as the Cape of Storms. This was some eight years after Jan van Riebeeck first arrived in 1652 to plant a food garden for the East India Company's passing ships beneath the towering heights of Table Mountain. Jan Pieterszoon Louw was given land next to the Liesbeeck River and – despite raids by local tribesmen, not best pleased to have their immemorial hunting rights trampled on by this new arrival – he made a success of his farm. He also had to contend with the depredations made by wild animals which roamed here: elephant, hippopotami, lions and leopards, to name but a few. He became one of the first successful Free Burghers to produce wheat at the Cape, later a staple of the colony. So the staff of life runs in my veins; no wonder I love every kind of bread.

I describe the Salt River Market as a food circus and it was. The calls of the Cape Coloured market stallholders were ribald, outrageous, flattering, and ultimately persuasive; they knew their customers intimately. They were brilliant ringmasters to the colourful goods on display, which included intricately cut watermelons that overwhelmed you with their sweet scent as slices were held out for you to taste. The red and green colours of this fruit, like a traffic light, stopped you in your tracks, even as the intoxicating smells of crushed fruit, spice and flowers urged you on.

'Merrem Merrem, ah beautiful lady, come and look at what I have kept just for you, the best, the sweetest, the loveliest watermelon, just like you. Don't break my heart, Madam, stop, stop, and have a little taste. *Kom proe soe bietjie.* Come and taste a little. Your lovely boy is wanting some I can see.' And, of course, I did want some, more than some.

After reserving a huge watermelon that had been knocked on for us to hear the hollow sound of a good ripe one, the very 'brother' of the one cut open next to it, we moved on through the cacophony. It was like walking into a scented rainbow. Flower stalls offered bunches of elegant white arum lilies, the whole range of *fynbos* flowers from pin cushions to proteas and roses of every shade, daisies, petunias, strelitzia, crane flowers and, trucked in 1,000 miles from Natal, blood red, white and pink anthuriums like waxed platters alongside every shade of orchid. Beside this sub-tropical display were the fruits of that region, pawpaw, mangoes, avocadoes, pineapples and lychees. The place was as much a crossroads of Africa and the world as were the spice merchants who also had a place here with heaped mounds of curry spices and coriander in every shade imaginable.

As an education in everything that was good to eat, there could not have been a better school. And you laughed and smiled as you wafted through this magic kingdom among the apples and pears, the cling peaches and the sugar-sweet nectarines whose flavour begged for marriage with goat cheese.

It was summer and I was in shorts and sandals and a short-sleeved shirt in a time before T-shirts. And here, in this place, summer was made manifest. Here you could inhale, smell, touch ('not too hard, Madam!') taste and eat summer itself.

As the stallholders packed up my mother's purchases, they would admonish her not to be a stranger and to remember who had given her the best deal, the best quality, the best fruit. They would smile and laugh and tease, gold teeth glinting. And they would shout at their competition to leave the lady alone, she was their customer.

Here, too, in gleaming displays that assaulted the nostrils was the harvest of the sea. Piled high in tubs of sea water were crayfish still moving, salt cod, sardines, fresh, dried and smoked snoek, kabeljou, kingklip, hake, yellowtail, and tunny in thick purple chunks. There were jars of pickled onions and vats of yellow pickled fish. And hanging in bunches, the scent winners with their knockout punch, were the wind-dried mullet, harders, known as bokkoms that my father loved. My mother would select the fattest smoked snoek, maybe some red herrings, some fresh harders and a sizeable chunk of yellowtail. And the bokkoms of course, which would stink up the car on the way home, fighting with the fruit for smell supremacy.

Our driver-gardener, Pieter Brill, would be in attendance and by the time we left, he and my mother would be weighted down with bags of fruit and vegetables. If there was too much, one of the stallholders would offer the help of one of his assistants with a wheelbarrow. Everything would then be carefully transferred into our car boot, being sure not to bruise any of the fruit.

How different was this market visit to that of my Jewish grandfather, made in 1890, when he first arrived penniless at the Cape to join his two brothers who had gone ahead from a small *shtetl* town near Vilnius in Lithuania, part of the Tsar's Russian empire. This ruler had decreed that Jews from the age of 18 to 40 would serve twenty years in his army. It was the last straw for many, and the exodus began that would take Jews to America, to Africa and to Australia.

Herman Raf was so hungry and so penniless that when he first walked the flower and vegetable strewn market aisles, he would beg the pickled herring seller to allow him to dip his finger into the briny barrels of silver fish to get the merest hint of a taste of this Eastern European delicacy; he was that hungry. How amazed he would have been to observe his grandson, 60 years later, wafted home in a large black Buick, crammed with the best the market could provide.

Once this cornucopia was unloaded and washed at home in Newlands it would disappear into the pantry and fridges and into fruit bowls which would need a Van Gogh or Paul Gauguin to capture them in paint, or maybe the local still life specialist, Irma Stern, who lived nearby in Rondebosch.

Shortly after our return, lunch would be served and it may well have been fried fish with Mrs Ball's Chutney and a salad, fresh bread from Enterprise, my father's bakery, with salted butter, followed by a sub-tropical fruit salad.

My younger sister Jay nicknamed me 'Apple-Boy' because of my love of apples. I had chosen a favourite food wisely in a house where the pantry held six or more cake tins filled with an assortment of biscuits, buttermilk rusks (one of my all-time passions), chocolate cake, coffee and walnut cake and a four-pound slab of fruit cake from the bakery. The pantry shelves groaned with jars of green figs in syrup, canned peaches and apricots and an array of dried fruit, meebos sweetmeats and huge fat raisins still on the stalk. Also in the biscuit tins were *kolwyntjies* (madeleines studded with currants), Hertzog cookies and always biltong and droewors (dried beef and sausage). How it is that at 71 I have not already died from diabetes is a miracle.

My mother was a feeder on a grand scale and at our groaning mahogany dining table many a slim girlfriend would come to grief in the years ahead. If the poor girl opted for chicken instead of beef my mother would ask, 'You don't like our beef?' And when the girl frantically denied this, she would hear, 'Then I will give you a small piece on the side to taste.' In the end my sister Jay, who had a lighter touch, would serve up for girlfriends who were grateful for this kindness.

I did not realise it at the age of five. but my palate was being educated in the best way possible. And I was making a meal of it.

CHAPTER 2

SUNDAY NIGHT SUPPER

In my family, growing up, we had a Sunday night tradition of a very simple meal after the huge Sunday lunch. So it would be sardines on toast with a poached egg, or we would get supper from my father's bakery. It was a great way of dispelling the impending gloom of homework not done and the horrors of the coming school week. For the last hour of the weekend, the coming reality could be put on hold as we drove to collect the meal at the factory and enjoyed what we had gathered there.

The factory was a large industrial operation called Enterprise Bakery and it ran 24/7. The place never slept. Hunkered down over a 20-acre site, its concertina roofline was a feature of Lansdowne in the 1950s and 1960s, when the area was still partly rural. It featured the longest rotating conveyor belt in Africa at the time, a wood-slat affair some quarter of a mile long on each side. Its job was to cool the oven-hot loaves to a temperature in which they could be stacked and loaded into wire mesh cubicles just behind the three dozen bright yellow Thames Trader trucks lined up in front, which would carry their cargo of bread and cakes to supermarkets and corner shops across Cape Town and way beyond to farming communities within a 40-mile radius first thing in the morning.

The delicious smell of baking bread, some thousands of loaves an hour, would greet us at a half mile's distance from the factory and my mouth would begin to water.

Our Sunday night food run to the bakery would garner a hoard of hot steak and kidney pies, donuts, iced Copenhagens, warm rolls and bread. Once bagged up and safely in the car, we would head home, each of the three children clutching a hot steak and kidney pie fresh from the oven, so much better than any reheated pie would ever taste. They were so hot it was impossible to eat them right away. You had to nibble at one end of the crust to make a small hole and then grasping the pie firmly, hold it out of the car window so that the rushing air could find entry into the pie through the hole and cool it sufficiently so that you could eat it. Greed often got the better of us and we'd arrive home with burned mouths, but as we got older this happened less and less as we knew from experience just how long to hold the pie out of the window, and as it cooled maybe nibble a larger gap in the pie's side and then back out the window again for some further cooling.

The wait would only add to the anticipation of devouring it and when it was finally just nicely warm, I would lie on the shelf below the rear window and enjoy it, in those happy days before safety belts had been thought of and when parents were rather more cavalier about child safety in cars.

The crisp outer layer of the pie was delicious, as was the soft steamed bottom of the pie lid, and then the deep mahogany-brown meat gravy was a taste sensation to a hungry child after a day in the swimming pool or at the beach. We would eat carefully, not wanting to lose any of the deliciousness but inevitably, meat gravy would run down our chins. At home we would need our faces and hands washed and the car seats would be sponged down, and then it was into the bath with us and afterwards straight to bed.

In our teens this Sunday ritual would continue but we were better able to control our need to gobble the pies straight away. Sitting down to the meal at home we would add tomato sauce to the dish, but in fact this did not add to the pleasure, and it changed the taste of the pie too. Some food is meant to be eaten straight from the hand, hot and fresh and so good you want to devour it.

I remember that feeling the first time I ate a hot lamb doner kebab with tomato, lettuce, red onion and tzatziki with a cold beer on the Greek Island of Skopelos. The level of satisfaction was much like those childhood pies, cooled in the Cape wind whistling through the car windows and the hot meat filling running down your chin. Bliss.

But bliss or not, Monday morning had to be faced and it was with a hollow gnawing fear in the pit of my stomach that I went off to school with some or all of my homework not done. How I survived school remains a mystery to me. I am indebted to this day to classmates who allowed me to hastily copy a version of their homework before school started, to ward off the worst teacher reprisals. But often enough I found myself sitting in detention or facing another caning from the headmaster. Looking back, I cannot understand why I did not simply do my bloody homework and be done with it and this regular Monday morning horror, but the truth is I lived in some kind of weird denial about the need to be educated and the more the teachers' wrath descended on me, the greater was my stubbornness not to comply with their wishes. It was a form of assured self-destruction which in time was visited on me with two standards failed and the need to repeat a year. The second time this happened, my long-suffering parents decided on a change of school and here I found like-minded misfits, square pegs in round holes and teachers adept at dealing with us, and I experienced a late mini-flowering of belated and limited academic success.

But this experience of Sunday nights of feasting on pies and Monday mornings of sackcloth and ashes at school has stayed with me. Even now, some sixty years later, I still get some echo of that anxiety on a Sunday night. But my passion for pies remains as steadfast as ever.

Chapter 3

Two Jars of Sour Fig Jam

It was 1962 and I was a gangling 12-year-old boy, getting close to the six foot two height I would be in a year or two, painfully shy and short-sighted and at a loss about who I was. Other people made me nervous.

I found myself once more at our cottage on the coast at Bloubergstrand for the summer holidays. The place, just 17 miles from Cape Town, was a ying and yang kind of village. On a still summer day it was paradise but when the howling South Easter, the 'Cape Doctor', got up to full rage, it was misery itself. The sea would turn a soul-deadening green-brown topped with whitecaps and I preferred to stay inside on those days to avoid the sandpapering effect of the wind-whipped sand that whined across the streets and beaches at shin height.

I found myself there rather than at our home in oak-bound Newlands, in the lee of Table Mountain, because of the continual series of chest infections that would, by the age of 13, send me and my lungs to the Karoo to dry out. A friend of my father, Dr Atta, from Malmesbury, had a cottage at Blouberg and suggested to my father that he too should build there, as the sea air would do me good. And so my scarred lungs and I found ourselves in Blouberg each summer and it must be said that the sea air cure must have worked for I am writing this at the age of 71 after four decades in the deep damp of the English climate.

Blouberg's strangeness was not limited to its microclimate but to its political temperature as well. The place was the summer home of many farmers from the Durbanville, Malmesbury, region and a more narrow-minded, racist bunch it would be hard to imagine. They gathered each Sunday at the small Dutch Reformed Church that went up behind our house with a piece of waste ground between, acting as a sort of *cordon sanitaire* from our Jewish Afrikaans weirdness. In church they sang their hymns to racial purity and listened to blood-curdling sermons of the waiting hellfire for any who dared to stray from the white fold. It was hugely ineffectual sermonising for the product of love on the wrong side of the blanket, the Coloured servants who staffed their homes, and ours, were all around us, ministering to our every and most intimate needs, albeit secretly and shamefully. Now and then a scandal would rock the place, when one of its leading lights would be found in bed with a brown servant girl, or worse, become the father of a brown bastard. It was not the most forgiving of places, and yet it accommodated itself to these lapses not too uncomfortably.

Almost lost in the dunes behind the village was a small whitewashed thatched cottage that had seen better days. It sat askew in the sand, as its rudimentary foundations must have moved when the singing sands shifted over the years. There was an air of bereavement, of abandonment, about the place. Its whitewash peeled and its thatch was untidy, and no one was ever seen outside it or at one of its tiny windows. It might well have been abandoned, but in fact it was home to the Kirstens, a brother and two sisters who were living testimony to the ill that befell those who in an earlier time had strayed from the all-white path. Though they were innocent of any wrongdoing, the sins of their father had been laid at their door. The siblings were nominally white but with just enough of the 'touch of the tar-brush', as the colloquial expression had it, to put them literally beyond the pale.

I was nervous of them and their cottage, as I was about

so much in my life, and yet I was a regular visitor. I had a small bay pony named Duke who lived in a lean-to shelter close to this cottage, which was most appropriately named *Die Muisnes*, 'The Mousenest'. The place seemed haunted. Today it is the site of the tallest building for miles around, a tower block of flats, and the old cottage lives on only in my mind and nowhere else.

Once a day I would go to see Duke to top up his water in his stable lean-to and in the half drum water butt in his sandy field, and to give him a net of alfalfa hay. I always kept a weather eye out for the Kirstens, but very seldom saw them. The old boy was thin to emaciation and the sisters were opposites: one was stout and one was the tiniest wisp of a woman. All were in their seventies, I guess, at the time, and they seemed ancient to me. Now and then, I would spot one or both of the sisters with small wicker pannier baskets, off foraging, for what I had no idea.

Now and then I would be forced to screw my courage to the sticking place and actually knock on their front door with its small round curtained window. A face would appear, always one of the sisters, usually the larger one, with her dark facial moles sprouting hairs and her steel grey hair pulled into a tight bun. I would be on an errand from my father, who included the Kirstens in his Christmas largesse, a four-pound tin of assorted biscuits and a slab of white iced Christmas fruitcake decorated with silver holly. The door would creak open, and a weird fusty smell would emanate from the dim corridor in which Miss Kirsten would be standing. She was the nearest thing to a witch I ever met in my childhood, right down to a cackling laugh. She would take the gifts from me and invite me in for a drink which I never accepted, always making my excuses, more gifts to deliver, and I would be off. I wonder now if she saw my fear. I expect she did. While I stood at her door, I felt bewitched, my feet stuck in glue, though I longed to escape.

They were harmless and the gentlest of souls, but it took me many more years before I was in my twenties and I could see them more clearly.

About a week or two after I had made my Christmas delivery to '*Die Muisnes*', we would see the three Kirsten siblings walking down Stadler Road towards our house. They would be got up in their best Sunday finery, clothes of a bygone age, a time long past, looking like the black and white photographs from an album of Victorian images that had some faint colour added to the cheeks. The old boy walked ramrod straight, as if on army parade. He would be in a fusty black suit, a khaki shirt and a dark tie, and the sisters, both large and small, in granny-print dresses that reached to their ankles, with feet in stout black shoes. They were an anachronism among the holiday-clothed residents and visitors spending a day at the beach, of whom the Kirstens seemed unaware, walking in their own time, their own reality, ghosts stranded in the mid-twentieth century. One of the sisters carried a wicker basket with a cloth covering.

Our servants would titter behind their hands as these three apparitions approached our front door. I would want to scarper, but some latent sense of good manners held me in a vice-like grip, and I usually stayed for the visit, which was conducted with all the stilted formality of an exchange of gifts between a wealthy landlord and some homage-paying peasants. There was, in this annual visit, something passing strange that went beyond my limited understanding but was all too evident at the same time.

It was only years later that I came to understand that these people were distant, *very* distant, it was stressed, relations of my mother who had Kirsten blood in her own veins, good Norwegian blood which had mixed wrongfully with some Cape Coloured family to produce these three siblings who had been banished to this wind-scoured landscape to seek redemption or to die. Within them, they held in their very being the central fascination and horror of miscegenation which so bedevilled our society. Their brief presence in our home for a formal cup of tea and polite stilted conversation, was clouded by an incubus of horror: something utterly beyond the pale had entered beneath our roof. By the time the handing over of their own gift came to be made, with all due formality, I was a nervous wreck.

They had brought the only gift that they could: their good manners and a jam made from the fruit of the sour fig succulents which grew in the sand dunes around their cottage.

It was a gift that spoke of the biblical window's mite. There was something sad and strange and defeated and mysterious about them. They seemed to come from another planet, another time. But their old-world manners and pride was also evident.

From the basket, beneath the tea towel covering, would be drawn by the larger Miss Kirsten, two glass jars of dark brown sour fig preserve, which my mother received with graciousness and thanks. Then the Kirstens rose and made their farewells and left. The jam was the result of their foraging sand dune walks, to harvest what they could.

Their gift joined others from previous years, untouched and untasted. The shame of it haunts me to this day.

CHAPTER 4

ARMY BLUES - STAFF OF LIFE

I was standing guard for the graveyard shift from 3am to 6am, on the first floor of a round concrete guard tower, which commanded views over the windswept wastes of Wingfield Airport in the middle of a Cape winter. It was an icy cold three hours, even bundled up in a balaclava, long johns, overalls, jersey and army greatcoat, thick socks and rubber-soled boots. It was 18 May 1971, my 21st birthday, and I was not best pleased to be there for my annual army camp. So close to home, yet so far away.

The night was pitch black and a fog lay thick over the airfield, turning the orange perimeter lights fuzzy. It was a fool's errand standing guard up there, but it had to be done. I shifted from foot to foot and counted my grievances against the army. It was a very long list.

For a much-indulged white boy it was not a bad corrective to a life of great comfort and privilege. But at the time I was not wise enough to see that or understand it. The hangars at this airport held one or two old Dakota workhorse planes and not much else. The Douglas C-47 Skytrain or Dakota (SAAF designation) was a military transport aircraft developed from the civilian Douglas DC-3 airliner. It was used extensively by the Allies during the Second World War and remained in front-line service with various military operators for many years, including the South African Air Force. It was the flying equivalent of the five-ton Bedford truck that I had learned to drive in the army.

It was the middle of the apartheid era in South Africa, even before the arrival of sin-inducing television. The political landscape looked as bleak as this godforsaken wind-eaten military airport.

I moved from foot to foot, did little limbering up jogs to keep warm and now and then ran up and down the echoing concrete steps to the ground floor and back up to my eyrie. My mind took me fishing, riding, dancing, eating out, and to thoughts of my then girlfriend tucked up in her bed not five miles from where I stood freezing my bollocks off. Fuck it.

The 13-pound weight of my FN 7.62 rifle weighed down whichever shoulder it hung from and so soon enough I leant it against the wall, keeping an ear out for any officer who might just be stupid enough to decide on an inspection visit to check up on the guard troop this icy night, on the lookout for dozing men.

Time dragged, not measured out in coffee spoons – there was no coffee on offer, nor any spoons. Rather the night was measured out by trying to see anything in the blackness or underneath the orange soda lights, or to check if I could see the outline of Table Mountain. And keeping away from any chink that let in the icy scalpel of the north wind, which howled and whined around the guardhouse like a maddened wolf.

God, I wanted to be out of there, away from Wingfield, away from the army and in bed with my girlfriend. Thoughts of her seemed totally improbable in that army gulag in mid-winter. She might just as well have been a ghost, a phantom. The minutes dragged by, the hours crawled. All feeling left my gloved hands and my booted feet. I was turning into an icicle.

And then, as the end of my three hours of guard duty crawled nearer, I noted an almost imperceptible lightening of the sky in the east. There was going to be another day after all.

At 6am I looked out for my replacement and heard his footsteps on the concrete stairs. We mumbled greetings and I made my way down to the ground. The sense of release and relief was palpable. I kicked my boots against one of the white painted rocks that marked the border of the path back to the guardhouse. My plan was to catch forty winks before breakfast at 7am. And then I saw headlights heading my way and a white van motored up to the front of the small redbrick arrivals and departure building which also housed a kitchen where rudimentary meals and sandwiches were prepared for the infrequent passengers.

I stopped and watched a small middle-aged Coloured man get out and open the back of the van where he filled a tray with loaves of bread. All thoughts of sleep vanished and I jogged over to him; the smell of freshly baked warm bread that wafted out of the van was utterly bewitching. I asked him if I could buy a loaf and wordlessly he took my money and gave me a small loaf of white bread, square and warm. I thanked him and took off my gloves to better get the bread's warmth onto my hands. I held it against my cheeks and inhaled that holy smell, almost as old as mankind.

The wind had dropped and as the sun rose. I found a sheltered spot behind the red brick building where the sunlight fell on a low wall. I leant my rifle against the wall and slowly tore off small pieces of the bread and ate it, savouring each mouthful. I lifted my face to the sun and was filled with a sense of joy and gratitude at this early birthday present, the best of all those I would receive once the camp ended and the only one that I remember today some fifty years later.

After I had finished the loaf to the very last crumb, I went into the kitchen and made myself a cup of milky instant coffee which I sipped and warmed my hands on. The mist was rising and melting before the sun and I felt happy. I made my way back to the guardhouse and lay down on my cot among my platoon, who were beginning to stir. I pulled the rough blanket over me and lay there fully dressed, filled with content. I would give the congealed breakfast porridge a miss this morning. Few meals can compare with that loaf of bread, the memory of which has fed me for 50 years and that still makes me smile to this day.

CHAPTER 5

EAGLE'S NEST BARBECUE

In my mid-20s, I lived for two years in a small cottage on the Eagle's Nest Estate, just below Constantia Nek in Cape Town. It was a magical place to call home. The property was owned by the Maggs family, who let out a couple of cottages on the place, one of them used by a horse-riding friend. When she moved on, I managed to rent the cottage and moved in myself around 1975.

I knew the place well as I used to drive up to Eagle's Nest to visit the brilliant potter, Hyme Rabinowitz, whose workshop was based at the top of the farm. He produced work that I loved, huge round bowls that looked wonderful heaped with fruit and came in blues and cobalt and earthen shades. To me they offered a ceramic style that was pure Africa. The work excited me, as did Hyme, who was one of those rare originals, a man of the spirit but also very much of the earth. After each visit and each purchase I felt that I had been given so much more than just another pot.

During this time, before I had discovered writing, I worked for my father's bakery, Enterprise, as a biscuit salesman. My beat included both supermarkets and Indian corner shops and small superettes. Although I was an adequate salesman, I did not find the work congenial and I was hugely conflicted about my life and my future. And added to this was a great unhappiness about the political reality of South Africa at the time. This concern peaked each year when it came time for me to do another army camp. I would prepare for it by getting fit, running up the hill from Constantia Village to the top of Eagle's Nest, a steady climb all the way on the estate.

I had a horse, Xanthus, stabled nearby, a deep red chestnut thoroughbred, with whom I would roam Tokai and the slopes of the Constantiaberg and Table Mountain itself, which I accessed at the Constantia Nek roundabout, on a gravel road used by the fire services.

It was a life of great privilege, made evident to me each working day as I traversed some of Cape Town's wealthiest suburbs and some of its poorest too. Enterprise biscuits were not that expensive, and they sold well everywhere. I should have been happy, I had so much to be happy about, but I was deeply troubled about my place in this society and working for my father, when I had little direction or insight as to my own true vocation. I did not wish to be a biscuit salesman. But I worked and ran, and went horse-riding, and dated girls and did all those things that privileged white boys in their twenties did, and it left me dissatisfied and conflicted.

Eagle's Nest provided a sort of refuge from my working life. When I drove through its entry gates at around 6pm of an evening I felt embraced by the woods and sheltered by the looming mass of Table Mountain that I could see over the tops of the swaying pinewoods that surrounded the cottage I called home.

I had a ritual during summer evenings when I got home. I would have a shower and then in fresh clean clothes I would go into the woods to collect dry fallen pine cones beneath the trees. Once I'd filled a horse feed sack full to bursting, I would stack them in the brick barbecue outside the cottage mixed with a handful of pine needles and have a fire going in seconds. Then, beer in hand, I would make a mixed salad with crisp lettuce, cucumber, avocado and blood red tomatoes. whose scent was closer to that of fruit than veg. I'd butter some fresh bread and take it all with the meat, lamb chops or boerewors or sometimes chicken, out to the fire. As I waited for the pine cones to burn down, I had a few minutes to take in that incomparable view of the mountain and some sense of peace would gradually work its way into me.

Then, with the fire a maze of fine red coals and hot ash, I would place the meat on the grid and after a few turns it would be done to perfection, salted and peppered, crisp and smoky on the outside, but still rare and succulent within. Then a second beer and, sitting by the still smoking fire I would eat slowly, savouring the meal.

Those weekday barbecues fed more than my stomach. They were in some indefinable way a confirmation of my simple humanity, my right to be there, a link with the earth and the pinewood. There was something sacred about them as well as profane, for I ate with appetite. I have always loved salty foods and sweet things too, and so I would end the meal with a piece of fruit or a slice of cake from the bakery, and a coffee. And by the time I had finished my meal I would feel more myself, like a diver who had come up from the depths and decompressed.

I smoked cigarettes or small cigarillos at that time, and I would light one then and inhale the smoke deep, watching the light fade on the mountain slopes, seeing the wisps of my barbecue fire disappear into the trees and the scent of the meat on the griddle would waft across the small lawned garden. Each of these outdoor meals was memorable for its simple delicious ingredients.

Looking at that majestic mountain vista, the words of a psalm would come to my mind: 'I will lift up mine eyes unto the hills, from whence cometh my help. My help cometh even from the Lord, which hath made heaven and earth. He will not suffer thy foot to be moved: he that keepeth thee will not sleep. Behold, he that keepeth Israel shall neither slumber nor sleep.' And truly something of the spirit of those words would reach me profoundly and ease for a moment whatever it was that was troubling me.

As I sat there, one of my interests would rise in my mind. The men and women who had made this place home before me, those who had lived here before the white men arrived from Holland, the San Bushmen and the Hottentots. How had it been for them? What did they eat? How did they feel about the sacred mountain? They were not great in stature, but well adapted to this place, hunter-gatherers. I could so easily imagine them coming through the pines, drawn by the lamb-scented smoke, to join me at my fire.

In the coming years I would attend many a braai, the cornerstone of South African life, the very heart of hospitality, friendship and entertaining. But few could match my solitary braais. These others were more about male camaraderie and beer than about anything else. And for my taste, I preferred my own food. Those Eagle's Nest braais were some of the best meals of my life. They sustained me during a troubled time when I was being grilled medium rare by life, for all the spice that I was given. You cannot ask much more of a pine cone fire and a lamb chop, can you?

CHAPTER 6

EATING GREECE

Eating grease is not healthy in anybody's book, but eating Greece is good for you.

My love affair with Greece began on a whirlwind tour of Europe that my family did when I was 20, my sister Janine, 18, and our brother Herman, 15. One of the standout food memories was in a restaurant situated just below the Acropolis, which was spotlit on a moonlight summer night in June 1970. Among the dishes we were served was something not particularly Greek but made Greek by its local additions – smoked salmon topped with diced sweet onion, capers and chopped hardboiled egg. It was a revelation of tastes.

Later, I would find the books and writings of Elizabeth David, who opened the eyes of the English-speaking world to the joys of Mediterranean food and Greek cooking in particular. She would write of going into an Athenian restaurant kitchen and savouring the sight and smells of the dishes cooking in 'enormous shallow pans', tomatoes and pimentos and zucchini blending into 'the marvellous smells which assail one's nose, and the sight of all those bright coloured concoctions is overwhelming. Peering into every stewpan, trying a spoonful of this, a morsel of that, it is easy to lose one's head and order a dish of everything on the menu.'

She found a small cottage in the village of Vari on Syros's southern coast, where she wrote about the abundance and variety of local ingredients which she used in her cooking. Her kitchen would be stocked with fresh bread, olive oil, olives, salt fish, hard white cheese, dried figs, tomato paste, rice, dried beans, sugar, coffee and wine. Fresh vegetables and fruit were obtained from the garden of the local tavern owner. She would write that while meat was available on special occasions, fresh fish would be brought to her regularly by a local fisher boy, from small fry or inkfish to occasional treats of langoustines and the famed Aegean *barbounia* (mullet). It was this exposure to good quality, simple ingredients which would become the hallmark of Elizabeth's recipes and writing.

So olives and olive oil became a staple of my own kitchen, coarse sea salt, aged balsamic vinegar, lemons and more lemons. I already knew the difference between a properly sun-ripened tomato and the tasteless supermarket varieties grown in Dutch polytunnels. My boyhood in the Cape had given me an educated palate that appreciated *geur*, the Afrikaans word for flavour, be it in a tomato or a melon, a cling peach or a nectarine.

My love affair with Greece deepened considerably when I stumbled across *The Magus* by John Fowles, a book set in Greece. And then the walking tour trilogy of Europe in the 1920s that brought Patrick Leigh Fermor to the Mani in Greece where he built a home and wrote so powerfully and passionately of his adopted country. These two writers both filled my kitchen store cupboards and primed the pump of my own wish to write of travel, landscapes and food. And I read *Gates of the Wind* by Michael Carroll, who sailed into Panormos Bay on the island of Skopelos, tucked his boat into the little inlet near the long beach and made this beautiful place his home.

Everyone has their favourite Greek island. Ours is Skopelos. In the mid-1980s we started to explore our new continent, Europe, and fell in love with the Greek islands. It's not hard to do. And with us it was love at first sight. The heat, the quality of the light and, on Skopelos, that combination of green trees and turquoise sea, took your breath away. Skopelos, loosely translated phonetically into my mother-tongue, Afrikaans, means kick free. The name proved prophetic.

Besides its ravishing beauty, the friendliness of its residents and their laid-back approach to life made it special. It was not on the major tourist map either. There was a handful of Germans, Scandinavians and Brits who had done their homework.

To get there, you fly into Skiathos, as Skopelos has no airport, one of the reasons it remains unspoiled. As you come in to land on Skiathos you cross a stretch of islet-dotted mauve, turquoise, cobalt and green sea, and then you are down. A brief bus transfer takes you to the little port where a Blue Dolphin hydrofoil whisks you in an hour to Skopelos Town. The thrust of massive engines lifts the craft to skiing speed in an instant, kicks up a white arabesque of spume and soon you are approaching that magic destination that tumbles down a steep hillside to its harbour. It is an exhilarating way to start a holiday.

From the quay at Skopelos, there is a taxi to your holiday apartment. A quick unpacking, then collecting a scooter or jeep that will be your holiday transport and you are sorted. In T-shirt and flip-flops, with bathing costume under your shorts, it's off to Limonari beach for a first swim. Having left Gatwick at 8am, with luck and a fair wind you will be in the water by 4pm.

That first drive through the orchards and forests over the island's mountain spine is a joy as warm air caresses you, sunshine warms your back, scents assail you, and lover-like, the island enfolds you and whispers 'Welcome back.'

The view that greets you as you come in alongside the coast on the far side of the island, seen from the high mountainside road, is one of the most beautiful that I know. It is a combination of intense blue sea and luminous green woods, offshore islands, small fishing boats and the distant mountains across that antique sea, all held in a light so pure it sings. You are in the land of Homer, of Helen and Jason of the Golden Fleece, of gods and heroes and poets. This place is part of a literary tradition that has inspired writers for millennia, and its impact on us that first time, after five years under grey English skies, was enough to make me pull the jeep over onto the gravel verge and like Cortes, look with a 'wild surmise, silent upon a peak in Darien.' We stood stunned by the sheer beauty that greeted us.

The Greek islands are receptacles of history. More so than other places, it seems to me. Maybe it is the beauty that calls in the power of spirit, leading to belief that the ancient gods are still at home here. They are certainly absent from the Acropolis in Athens, which is a human tour de force. However, in the hidden groves of Skopelos, you come closer to the spiritual power of that which is ancient and powerful. Up a mountainside in a deciduous forest, whispering in the wind, a bell-clonking chestnut herd of topaz-eyed goats comes round a corner and Pan is there too, as unseen as an artist's signature, but indisputably present in the image. In a secluded cove, all turquoise and green and shimmering heat, it is easy to imagine a dalliance between Neptune and Diana. Or a sacrifice. And as dusk sweeps in from the indigo sea and settles dark on the land, constellations of light reignite the sense of wonder. A chill brings goosebumps, and you turn round to look behind you, the hairs on your neck and arms raised.

Finding myself on a Greek island was seminal to my development as a writer. Here I was at last in this landscape of myth and magic, and the reality was as good as everything I had been led to expect. I understood why Paddy Leigh Fermor had made Greece his home these decades past, having crossed the whole of Europe on foot at the age of eighteen. Greece was where he had played his part in the Second World War, on Crete, capturing a German general. In the book about this saga, *Ill Met By Moonlight: The Abduction of General Kreipe*, by William Stanley Moss, Paddy's second-in-command, it tells how the general was devastated by his capture. But later this changed. One day, the general started to recite Horace's ode *Ad Thaliarchum*, and Leigh Fermor, a keen reader of Horace, took it up, reciting the rest of the poem. The two adversaries stared at each other and understood that they shared more than might have been obvious at first. Such is the power of Greece, ancient and modern, to unite the most unlikely people.

Limonari, the first beach on this side of the island, is little more than a cove with a solitary seasonal taverna. The sand is gold and flows into that gin-clear water. That first plunge into coolness is unforgettable. It is like getting into silk sheets after a hot bath. There is sensual overload and at the same time a cleansing, a putting away of London and your everyday world. You are now physically in the magic, down the rabbit hole, beyond the back of the wardrobe, into the bewitching garden. Beneath the surface the still, cool, azure silence and then the soft susurration of wave-rolled pebbles. The deep darkness beyond and the sunlight dapples on the surface. All of this enters your soul, and you emerge a different person to the one who entered the water earlier. It is as if you have shed six layers of skin and everything, every sense, is new and enhanced. The water runs down your body and you remember what it is to be alive and happy. And you would not wish to be anywhere else on earth.

As you slowly explore the island, the scenic coast road to Glossa offers beaches so beautiful that Hollywood chose them for *Mamma Mia*, the movie based on ABBA's songs, with Meryl Streep, Colin Firth and Pierce Brosnan. There is endless Milia, the tiny Andrines, unique Kastani, Hovolo, Limonari, Staphylos and Velanio, one of the island's loveliest beaches, a favourite with nudists and those who enjoy walking. On incomparable Panormos, our favourite, an evening dip is an unforgettable experience, swimming in what seems to be a river of gold as the sun sinks beneath the horizon.

In the weeks ahead, as one day slips seamlessly into another, an inner quietness comes to you, a calm that recharges the batteries. Each day adds its five-sided memories, sight-smell-touch-taste-hearing, adding up to more than the sum of the parts. Sleeping after lunch, in a room with shutters drawn and the scent of herbs on the hillside wafting through, the song of cicadas loud in the silence, one wakes with a sense of wonder and content. There is time to turn over the myriad riches of each day, a pantry of glowing bottled wealth that will stay with you and light dark winter evenings in England.

With the conscious shucking off of England comes the realisation that with courage and ingenuity this could be your home, that this scented earth with its freight of brooding ancients who lived, loved, fought and died here, could also be your place. That the cobalt sea, the triremes, the sagas and the myths, the woods and the villages, the sea-splashed rising and setting sun, this could be your neighbourhood. It is a bewitching thought, and some give in to it.

And, being Greece, food is a fundamental part of the pleasure. Here a restaurant's guests think nothing of walking into the kitchen to see what's cooking and there is a friendliness and unpretentiousness that takes the simple good things of the earth and the sea and sky for granted.

The first time I ate at a table and chair set in the sea, was a revelation. The swish of rippling wavelets about our feet was cool and enchanting, and the topsy-turviness of dinner in the water was a delight. And the food was good, making no compromises with the liquid setting. Fresh calamari, deep-fried, served with lemons from island trees, thick-skinned and fragrant, and a Greek salad, a thick slab of herb and olive oil drizzled feta cheese resting on succulent tomatoes, olives, cucumber, and finely sliced red onion. With it came warm chunks of pale yellow bread. We sipped our beer and retsina, aware of happiness served as a side-dish. As we ate, we dropped pieces of bread in the water, bringing in schools of small striped silver fish that made the shallows bubble as they jostled for food, some bolder than others gently nibbling our legs.

After supper, we drove to Skopelos town to promenade with the families on the quayside, sitting down for 'honey balls', ice cream, coffee, Metaxa brandy and a cigarillo. The small hot honey-coated doughnuts accompanied by vanilla ice cream and a black Greek coffee is a trinity as good as any, and that cigarillo, the perfect end to the day. A shower, clean sheets and sleep beckoned. Above, the night sky gleamed and pulsed clear of light pollution, the stars guests at our Greek banquet.

One day we discovered a simple restaurant in the garden of an old country house, some way outside the town. We were the only guests for lunch and we sat on rustic chairs under a tree in the sun-dappled shade. There was just one thing on the menu – chicken. But what chicken. It was a whole bird, cooked slowly in tomatoes, olives and herbs. The flavour of the maroon-red sauce was deep, pungent, intense, and we mopped it up with bread. The flesh fell away from the bones and each disbelieving mouthful demanded another. A simple Greek salad added a refreshing note that worked as a palate cleanser. We drank a dark, powerful wine served in a carafe. It was quiet except for the cicadas and having no shared language with our hosts, we were left in peace to get on with it.

That night, too full for supper, we opted for Greek yoghurt with honey, walnuts and sultanas. It was enough. A coffee rounded off another perfect day of eating Greek culture.

Much later, when hunger returned, we ate a warm, paper-wrapped shawarma and drank an ice-cold beer, standing under a plane tree in a small square, listening to bouzouki music, another unexpected pleasure. The lamb succulent and salty, caramelised at the edges, onions, salad and a garlic sauce folded into warm flat bread. The hours of swimming gave an edge to our appetite.

Each day would start with the utter luxury of sunshine and breakfast on the terrace overlooking the sea. Fresh bread or rolls from the baker in the village, butter, jam and coffee. Then the big decision of the day – which beach? Usually Panormos or Milia. Both were beautiful, and both had tavernas where we could lunch simply. A gentle drive of a few minutes, a place with an umbrella and sun lounger chosen and that was the day sorted. Hours of reading, sunbathing and swimming followed in an unhurried daze, seen through sunglasses. Wandering through this idyll were other couples or Greek families from the mainland, kids, young couples and grandparents, three generations content together, all lending a hand with the youngest.

There were beaches where you could be almost totally alone if you chose, with perhaps one other couple a few hundred yards off. There was no pressure, one could just be. A snooze after lunch under the umbrella or in the woods behind the beach and then that lazy, slightly dizzy walk into the water again, surfacing to stare at the mountains with their secluded chapels.

As six o' clock approached, we would collect our things and return to our place for a shower, then drive to Skopelos town to find a quayside restaurant for the evening buzz, eating simply, chops or kebabs or grilled chicken, all done over charcoal, salad and bread and baklava or yogurt and honey and coffee. Then home to bed. The unchanging routine mantra-like, each day a click on a string of unworried beads.

After a while, you began to pay more attention to the people of this place. The island population is a mix of the sophisticated and sons of the soil. Most people live in the towns on the island's coast, plain, pedestrian Glossa, and pretty romantic Skopelos town. There is a sprinkling of farms as well, but they are few and far between.

The locals are much in evidence. There are the cap-wearing old boys who gather at certain cafes and chat and smoke and play backgammon, or simply perch in lines on a quayside wall, like swallows preparing for flight, watching the world go by, happy, you suspect, to be out of the house and away from wives demanding chores. Elderly women are not seen in public much, black-clad figures glimpsed sweeping, shopping, visiting churches and chapels. These island people are unknowable to tourists and what they make of us is probably not a subject for mixed company. Hardship is written on their dark weathered faces, yet they carry a quality of quiet dignity with them.

At the other end of the spectrum, there are the vociferous, argumentative, opinionated, loud, dictatorial taxi drivers and shop owners of the commercial class, whose robust energy, cynicism, paranoia, and anger lie close to the surface, often disguised by smooth Levantine charm and chic clothes. Some of them run the best jewellery shops, art galleries and jazz clubs amid the whitewashed alleys and blue shutters that honeycomb this hill of humanity.

Here as dusk falls softly and lamps light the alleyways, sounds of Miles Davis and Duke Ellington bring something of New York to the Aegean. These shops offer goods to tempt sophisticated tastes, supple leather bags, French and Italian couture labels, antiques, carpets and art. There are shops that could be offshoots of Tutankhamun's tomb, so stuffed are they with antique and exotic jewellery, fine ceramics and sculpture, most made recently. Some, at eye-watering prices, are possibly genuine, or so you are told by the gallery owners. They proffer documents, readily to hand to prove provenance. Rumour has it that the country's Minister of Culture holidays here, which may be an endorsement for this trade – maybe, maybe not.

All of this, the poverty and hardship, the luxury and sophistication and the heart-stopping beauty, all of it makes up the complex fascination of this island's appeal. It is as hard to capture as the semi-wild cats that haunt the harbours, alleys and taverna tables, sharp of face and hip, and ever hungry. When not hustling, they are given to sun-washed snoozing, white, black, grey, brindled or marmalade, their pointed Nefertiti faces observe, evaluate and cajole, with nothing of servility about them, rather a certain supercilious air. It gets to you, this place.

One day, I stepped on a sea urchin. The pain was intense, and I hobbled into the rather ramshackle hospital. Language was suddenly a problem and the doctor brusque and hostile, plainly not a part of the tourist service. It was a shock and it made me reassess the dream of living on the island. It was as if my eyes were suddenly opened. Over the next week I spoke to waiters, shopkeepers, bakers, taxi drivers and asked questions. And it soon became clear that life here was hard. The beautiful sea was almost barren, farming an endless backbreaking grind for little reward, there was no industry. We, the tourists, were the only game in town, and that for only five months a year, Easter till the end of August, with maybe a few stragglers in September. By then, everyone on the island and those imported to help, were exhausted and tempers frayed. With autumn the island cleared, as most locals and summer workers made their way back to Athens to work through the winter until the tourists returned to the island at Easter. This jewellery box island place was locked up, closed down for business. The weather turned brutal with months of rain, and snow not unknown. This is why there are forests on this north Aegean Island. It is a thoroughly wet place in winter.

I read more, and discovered a history steeped in blood and suffering. The place had been invaded and settled by waves of conquerors, Spartans, Romans, the most recent being Turks, Italians and then the Germans in the Second World. Then came the Greek Civil War. I tried to imagine these pristine coves and beaches as the setting for war and found it impossible. Our paradise had human failings after all, and in some strange way this made the place more real. The toy taken out for summer fun was only half the tale.

Our holiday idyll was made possible by hard work and a sea transport infrastructure. Food had to be shipped in in industrial quantities, as well as beer, wine, petrol. The ferries were not simply transporting holidaymakers, they were carrying bricks and cement and steel for building.

And the setting for all this, the beguiling blue sea of gentle beauty, was also a mirage. This shallow sea is beset with reefs and has the capacity to turn violent suddenly as terrible winds whip up ship-eating waves. Wrecks strew the seabed. Little boats from pre-history to modern cargo ships have gone down here, gulped whole by this silky sea. A virago-like wind takes a dim view of complacency or romantic maunderings. It is an unforgiving place in the wrong mood.

And yet we returned, year on year. Eventually, we brought our children, and Skopelos found a place in our family narrative. Today, its food informs our cooking, we bear the physical scars of its rough edges, its sunshine and beauty inhabits our hearts and memories. It lies there at the top of the Aegean, waiting still, as it has through history. An emerald set in a sapphire sea. And we know that one day we will return, no longer young, hurt by life, and less romantic, and the island will beguile us yet again for it is all it ever was, but now it is also family, part of us.

CHAPTER 7

FISH FOR SUPPER

For Herman

There is an aroma that signals the end to a perfect day's fishing and which alerts your taste buds to a feast in the making – a 5lb winter-fed galjoen on a rooikrans wood fire, smoking and spitting fat.

That intoxicating scent of a fat galjoen on the barbecue takes me back to Hamerkop fifty years ago as if it was yesterday. The fish would be butterflied open from the back like a kipper, salted and peppered and placed on the griddle above the coals, skin side down to crisp first.

My brother Herman reminded me of it just recently, the happy end of a memorable day's fishing on this remote, wild coast in the Cape. We'd walked from our father's fishing shack at Hamerkop on the Bredasdorp coast, along the rockbound shore to a favourite angling spot at Monument Rock, to fish for galjoen. It was 1973. I was 23 and he was 18.

You reached this fishing paradise at Hamerkop along a rocky mountain track, using one of the two Second World War Willys Jeeps that our father garaged in a farm shed inland of the range of hills which separated the farm from the sea. The slow crawling ascent was rough enough to break a spring or an axle if you were not careful. It could take almost an hour to reach the cottage which, as the crow flew, would have been just three miles on the other side of the range of hills.

It was a place without people but not without animals; buck, baboon, snakes and one or two leopard were discreetly evident amid the flowering *fynbos* kingdom of proteas and pincushions, with some 260 bird species. Now and then, on a day with no wind, you would hear the bark of a baboon or the cough of a leopard, playing out the age-old dance of life and death between these ancient enemies who made their home in these coastal hills.

The line of green hills with its dense bush cover dropped steeply to the coast, concertinaed with kloofs. In these places were the cave homes of both leopard and baboon and the black mussel middens which were the mark of prehistoric man.

But for us the hills were of little interest once we crested their brow and the sea opened up before us, the Indian Ocean with thousands of miles of open water all the way to India and beyond, giving the waves sufficient fetch, as sailors say, to make this place a ship's graveyard, especially so when the wind and the currents were in opposition to each other.

The fetch and heft of these sometimes giant waves pounded the coast, beating the water into a double cream mix above the blue, the very conditions so loved by galjoen, that doughty fighter. Not for them the calm places or beach waters, no; for them the coast's rocky teeth and deep gullies were home. Having to fight just to stay alive made them worthy adversaries for an angler, and the slight metallic taste of their fine, white, black-veined flesh came as no surprise. When just landed, they looked like cast bronze, the black-green brown of metal.

It was good to have Herman's company. He was always upbeat, energised, optimistic, brave and crazy hungry to get his line in the water. I was rather more downbeat and mood-bedevilled, but the partnership worked and has lasted a lifetime.

That morning at Hamerkop started early with a coffee,

but no time for breakfast. We could hear the thunder of the surf breaking on the beach in front of the cottage and see the spray where it exploded on the rocks south of us at Lynkrans and just to the north at Monument Rock. And so we wanted to get going. Half an hour's walk in the dawn light would get us there on a faint rocky trail just above the beach, the stones flecked with orange lichen and the flick of lizard tails among the succulent sour fig plants and their as yet unopened pink and yellow mardi-gras coloured flowers. The scent of fynbos fought for supremacy with the iodine-laden sea air, making for an intoxicating cocktail.

There was a fierce male joy in us, in the thought of the day's fishing, in the deep bond between us, in the escape from our father and the civilities and incivilities of the fishing shack. And just below it, in me certainly, even then, the sure and certain knowledge that this would not last, that somehow this time would end badly for us and our benighted country, scarred by the genocide of apartheid, that in part had given us access to this utterly supreme gift, private ownership to ten miles of coast. This feeling added a bittersweetness to the day that made me want to savour it to the very dregs, to take it into me so deep that it would become part of me, of who I was as a person, and mark my bones like the work of Eskimos and those winter-stranded fishermen who carved narwhal tusk ivory and whalebone.

And that conscious willing of the place to enter my soul worked, for as I sit here now in England after forty years of absence from that coast, I hear the waves still, their thrum and crash, their hiss and suck, and feel its electric air and hear the baboons and feel the sea-fret upon my face and hands. The place is no longer ours; it was taken from us by government order and placed in public ownership as a nature reserve known today as De Hoop. It remains a sadness that the family lost it, but given its new role as a place for the regeneration of fish stocks, it is a loss that I, for one, can live with.

But on this day we were still innocent of what life held in store – siblings separated on two northern continents, Europe and America, with our sister still in Africa.

As always, when I was with him in those days and even

now, the 1969 song by The Hollies, *He Ain't Heavy, He's My Brother,* comes to mind.

It's a long, long road
From which there is no return
While we're on the way to there
Why not share

And the load
Doesn't weigh me down at all
He ain't heavy, he's my brother

But as it turned out, Herman did more of the carrying through our lives, and I was fortunate, for he was stronger than me and remains so.

We reached Monument Rock just as the sun rose out of the sea, in all its gold triumph, seemingly with an orchestration of brass horns, a challenge to the day ahead to be prepared for heat. It was still winter, but the rocks were instantly warm and the slick wet of the sea mist and the night's dew began to dry off the rocks on which we stood, good flat slabs of red brown, comfortable to fish from.

Although we could not see them, we knew well that around us in the pulsing, cresting seas were great pods of dolphins, seals, southern right whales and at least 250 species of fish. Each year between July and November, southern right whales make their epic journey back to the safety of these rich waters to mate and calve, a spectacular sight we were privileged to witness.

But on this day, it was galjoen only that interested us, and we made trace and baited up with alacrity. You did not have to cast far, as the rock on which we stood sliced fifty metres into the surf, but you had to be able to drop your bait and sinker just shy of the rock shoals and sentinel rocks that crested the water even at high tide.

With practiced ease, we began our day's fishing, casting and retrieving our line and testing the fish with a menu of redbait, white mussel and blue-green coral worm, which was fish dynamite of a kind.

Soon enough, the strikes began. These fish don't peck

and run, they attack the bait as if their lives depend on it and one whip back of your rod would set the hook fast, and then it was fight on. These fish were savvy and used the waves and the tide to give them every chance to pull back against our thrumming lines and straining rods that were buried into leather fighting saddles, fighting to escape to the rocks and reefs, where they could dive into crevices which would chafe the line to breaking in a split second.

Once the fish's initial wild runs were dampened and you began to bring it towards the rock on which you stood, you had to time its arrival with an incoming swell or risk losing it on the shelf of jagged reef just below the water's edge. This shelf boasted sharp black mussel colonies and banks of the leather breasts and erect nipples of redbait clumps which would squirt water back into the sea like 30 schoolboys taking a piss all at once. Experience had taught us how to play fish here, and in the course of the morning we had landed two or three each. Decent fish, all five or six pounds, and fat from good feeding in these food rich seas.

And then, just as suddenly as the feeding frenzy had begun, it would end, for reasons we never understood but accepted, given the bounty on the rocks.

We stopped to take stock, looked at the time and noted that it was noon. The morning had fled and we were sunburnt and hungry and thirsty.

We gutted and scaled the fish and threaded them onto heavy line, with each of us carrying his own catch, and headed back to the cottage for lunch.

That evening, after an afternoon nap and a long walk on the beach, the fish would be expertly braaied by Martin T'shila and Henry Vel, who made our father's fishing adventures into luxury expeditions. They would build a fire in the dusk within a halved 44-gallon oil drum so that the fish sat a good two foot from any flame and only when there was a bed of cherry red rooikrantz coals would the fish go on, two or three galjoen.

A cold Castle lager in hand, we would sit round the fire with them and chat about the morning's excitements, and tease and argue as to who had landed the biggest fish.

And then the moment when with plates loaded with

smoking savoury fish, buttered baked potato and a salad, we would eat in the flickering firelight, like gods feasting. And it was good, so good. I would go back now to that time and that place and halt the wheel of life just long enough to get one last fill of it, as it was then, for in many ways it was among the best, the very best that life has offered me.

The years would pass and our boyhood with it, and we would lose Hamerkop in the late 1970s and South Africa would lose us in 1980. But in some strange way, the wire-thread memory of that day would wind into others like it, to form a steel cable so strong that even though today we live separated by the 3,000 miles of the Atlantic and the 3,000 mile width of America, my brother and I remain connected, like two flies caught in amber that day at Hamerkop – and linked in love by the taste of that galjoen on the coals that we ate for supper.

CHAPTER 8

AUTUMN IN FRANCE

There is much to recommend a holiday in France after the frantic month of August. When France's national holiday month has come and gone and with it the millions of French and other tourists who swarm every square inch of recreational land in the country, I thought it might be the perfect time to visit once more. But France can be subject to moods.

September brings with it a return to normality and space and peace along the Atlantic and Mediterranean beaches as well as the inland resort areas, the beautiful hilltop *bastide* towns of the south-east and west, many of the most beautiful villages of Provence. Sanity returns.

Or so you would think. But think again. The whole of the tourist serving workforce is recovering from the shock of dealing with their own demanding tourists and the ignorant foreigners who don't speak their language, who invade each August from as far away as Sweden, Britain, Holland, Germany, Japan and the United States, asking for food and drink and beds with a greater or lesser degree of success in a babble of foreign tongues or mangled French. By September, the hotel and restaurant staff are knackered and just want to kick back a little and take it easy.

And then the pensioners and those old enough to know better arrive, thinking that they will have France gloriously to themselves now that the screaming hordes of kids are once more safely penned up in schools, their parents once more tied to the grindstone, all of France theirs to enjoy. But age does not always bring wisdom.

We drove down to the Lot from Sussex in a day of glorious, trouble-free motoring in my old Mercedes CLS which has the great advantage of sitting on motorways steady as a rock at 80mph. We'd emerged from the Channel Tunnel, blinking in the sunshine of this new France, a country reborn in May 2017 with a young charismatic leader, Emmanuel Macron.

As we drove ever further south and the traffic thinned to French levels, we stopped for food and coffee and rest breaks and noticed that the motorway fuel stops, which serve a superior cuisine to that found in British equivalents, were not as good as usual and the staff a tad abrupt. Not all, but some.

There was, too, the usual tension at *péages,* where you need to keep your wits about you when collecting tickets or paying with a debit card. Any hesitation, deviation or muddle will lead to hooting from behind you as your number plate advertises the fact that you are another bloody Brexiteer – one of the tribe of British turncoats, Perfidious Albion having once more shown its untrustworthiness.

Ah yes, for those of us who voted to remain there is the bitterness of a fresh dislike we really do not deserve but which we cannot defend ourselves against. You can see the thinking in more than a few eyes. 'Why are you here, if you voted to leave the EU?'

Our destination was a former winemaker's house in the Lot, just above the small village of Luzech, where the river makes a bow, doubling around the place so that it needs two bridges. We found the house at around 10pm in the pitch dark thanks to map coordinates plugged into the iPhone's GPS. We had enjoyed a leisurely dinner in a nearby bistro in Castelfranc – *magret de canard* once again, done on a fire right in front of us.

We were tired, having driven for 12 hours the 700

miles from home and coped with a mix of sun and rain and some violent storms. The house was in darkness, and it took us a good half hour to find where the keys were secreted, the scent of red damask roses and ripe figs all around us in the velvet soft night. An owl hooted welcome. Eventually we found the tower part of the property we'd booked after searching the whole house, made up our beds and collapsed into them for a dreamless eight hours.

After good showers the next morning, we set off to find breakfast in Luzech, not having had time to stop for groceries in our mad dash south.

The hills were alive with the sound of gunfire as the locals went in search of *sanglier*, the wild boar who infest the hundreds of square miles of *garrigue.* The boar were making hay while the sun shone down in the valley bottoms, feasting on corn and grapes and just-fallen acorns. Lezech was quiet, basking in the sunshine within the serpentine embrace of its river, and we found a café easily enough. The elderly owner pointed to a boulangerie over the road where we found perfect croissants, returning with our prizes to his excellent coffee.

Days of sheer pleasure followed as we toured the many beautiful villages, towns and valleys that make the Lot the tourist paradise that it is. We were not alone. Many other British visitors had patently had the same idea as us and filled the markets and restaurants with their subdued *sotto voce* chat. Many too were local residents, expat Brits, boosting the provincial economy by buying up ruins that the French were happy to hand over, preferring new-build homes themselves.

We noticed posters everywhere advertising the 'Miss Lot' beauty competition with a lovely blonde girl in a red dress decorating the poster. What would that be like we wondered, the old journalistic sense of a possible story still at work. We said maybe we'd go along to the local run-off in Luzech, but this aspect of local colour seemed too far off our radar and we gave it a miss in the end.

One morning we decided to drive over to Monflanquin, which we'd visited with our children many years ago. Back then it was *en fête* and the kids had the time of their lives, being invited to join a procession one evening to celebrate the local Catholic saint. Handed burning pitch torches, they were thrilled to be part of this strange foreign ritual that involved naked flames. Now the place was as deserted and shuttered as if a cowboy town was expecting the James Gang to ride in shortly, guns blazing. It was eerie. The only thing moving were autumn leaves blown across the empty squares and, in the central piazza, the slow chewing of British pensioners working through ham and cheese baguettes.

There seemed to be a sadness in these valleys as if, after a riotous party, just the wine glass dregs and the clogged cigarette ashtrays remained, a melancholy reminder of the celebration past.

We took refuge on the deck of a restaurant and asked for coffee. After an eternity the waiter laid the table with cutlery and serviettes and water. We said all we wanted was coffee when he returned. He said something rude sounding under his breath and cleared the table violently and rushed off. To my surprise Jan got up and walked out. I followed in her wake, looking nervously over my shoulder all the while. We found a new place which did crêpes, and the young French waitress could not have been nicer. Plum crêpes and cappuccino went down a treat, and there was no sign of the waiter from down the street.

You would think that finding a place to eat in France is akin to rolling off a log. But the villages seemed largely deserted, ghost towns along the river Lot, empty echoing architectural pearls glinting in the sun, with the occasional flurry of rain. There was a mournfulness about these places, a sense of better times long past. Empty because the young had fled agriculture and the peasant way of life for better-paid work in the cities. These old towns were now inhabited thinly by the elderly, a pale echo of their former bustling selves. As a consequence, it was hard to find a meal, with restaurants few and far between and these often closed at odd times, Mondays, Thursdays or any other day that took their fancy.

Now and then we struck lucky, and it made up for all the disappointments. We ate one lunch at the Le Pont Restaurant in Castelfranc and it was like going back to the 1980s. The place was rammed with a mix of locals including two workmen in vests, their high-viz clothing stashed by their feet, and a sprinkling of tourists like us. Madame was a tall blonde woman in her fifties with a smoky cigarette voice, her husband the chef in the kitchen. The menu du jour was 13.90 Euros for three courses. A salad tricolore or an egg mayonnaise salad, rabbit casserole or confit of duck or salmon in sesame sauce and dessert. It was excellent, served efficiently by a charming teenage English waitress whose parents had left Truro in Cornwall for Castelfranc ten years previously and who still did not speak French, though their daughter sounded absolutely French when she addressed the patrons in their own language. She loved the place, she said, and looked happy. We wondered at the journey she and her parents had taken; what had brought them here and how did they fit in?

After a post-lunch walk by the river, we went exploring again. And then there was the matter of navigation. Jan is a master at this. In fact, one could say that she has a doctorate in navigation, having taken us across Europe with a caravan in tow back in 1985 using a sheaf of Michelin maps, and never ever putting a foot wrong. Probably just as well, for back in those days I was rather more easily excited and quick to anger. Four decades of marriage have taught me to be less intemperate.

But now the good old days of maps are gone, and the dictatorship of GPS has invaded the car and matrimony itself. Jan is an early adopter of anything technological and is a whizz at it all. I have been a major beneficiary, as I am useless at anything to do with IT. So with her iPhone at the ready and maps tucked to one side we set off. The problem with GPS is that at any roundabout or crossroads it has a major meltdown, like a menu offering sixty things to eat, it wants to go in every direction at once and would like to know if one can order ten starters, but with no main and could the route to the next place be a pretty one with no cars on it? This does not bode well for happy travel, once off the motorway.

We went to visit Saint Cirq Lapopie, arguably one of the most beautiful villages in France. It is sighted breathtakingly above a curve of the Lot and its tall mediaeval buildings grace the landscape with a dream of how life could be if only one could afford a room in this most desirable of places. But unlike our early 1980s discovery of this charming place, it has now been discovered by others. You have to park a mile away and pay for the privilege. Then you must walk along a dangerous road to get close to the place and compete for space with a thousand other visitors all walking blind as they photograph their future memories. We did a U-turn and Saint Cirq Lapopie freezing pool that we'd been told was a heated facility. But we slept like the tired travellers we were, surrounded by a deep silence, only broken by the distant cry of a buzzard.

The next morning, we set off for Cahors market and found parking just seven minutes from the centre of town and its bustling market square. I bought six pearl-handled steak knives, promised to be dishwasher proof and so sharp one could shave with them. We bought some *jambon crû* and then some bread, and to finish our picnic shopping Jan said, 'Let's get some cheese.'

In the corner of the market a huge unshaven man was doling out wafer thin slices of cheese from a cartwheel sized object that was made of sheep's milk. The taste was sublime, sweet and tangy in one. Jan indicated a certain thickness, and a huge cutlass-like knife came down.

The slab of cheese was weighed and wrapped, and we were asked for £79 for an amount just over a kilo. Joint family meltdown. The ogre flipped open a plastic covered price tag, hidden till then, which read Euro 59 per kilo. Jan was ready to argue the toss and did, but to no avail. The ogre demanded my card and before we knew it, we were shamefacedly and angrily – both at the same time – trying to get away from the man while being weighted down by that pavestone slab of butter yellow cheese in its bag. I could feel the man's eyes on me, and he was saying: '*Le Rosbifs, zero, France dix*!'

Eventually, we found a small, scruffy place on the other side of the market with a young waiter who appeared to be high on something, maybe life. We ordered: Jan asked for the burger, no bun, with fries on the side. I ordered the cassoulet. The food and two glasses of robust red wine arrived in good time and was the real deal.

We felt that we had come to a good place after all. You can survive France in the autumn if you are brave and if you persist. I recalled the words of a Paris delicatessen owner where I had first been overcome with the best that France offered: *'Courage mon brave, courage!'* he'd said, patting me on the shoulder. How right he was, one needs to be brave at times travelling in France, especially in September.

CHAPTER 9

HOME GROWN

I've just eaten an apple from a tree I planted in our garden four years ago, a dwarf variety of Scrumptious. It was delicious. I peeled off the bright red skin with a potato peeler, and its surface layer was pink; beneath that it was creamy white. Its taste reflected its name. It certainly was scrumptious, sweet, with almost no hint of tartness, just a delicious flavour of honeyed lemon with the scent of honeysuckle. What a happy moment, to eat something you have grown yourself.

The little tree is heavy with small, round, bright red apples. A few have fallen for the enjoyment of the slugs and garden birds. It stands in the lee of a tall rowan tree that now, at the end of August, has already lost its berries to the feasting birds.

On the other side is another small apple tree I put in at the same time, producing Cox, much tarter and good for apple pies and apple sauce. And then finally, there is a Victoria plum tree which this year went crazy, producing so much fruit I have cooked and pureed the fruit with added sugar to go with ice cream as a dessert. Its colour and flavour are both winners. I added some to a sauce for barbecued pork ribs last night and its sticky sweet-sour consistency worked beautifully with the meat.

A few weeks earlier, at the tail end of June, I dug up three tubs of new potatoes. They took the prize this year for my garden's produce. Quite unlike any bought potato, they were simply washed and boiled and eaten with lashings of salted Brittany butter. Heaven on a plate. And so simple. When you eat something you have grown in the loam of your own garden, there is something almost sacred in the act.

All around us the woods, hedgerows and fields are producing a glut for foragers. The field mushrooms are everywhere in their fairy circles; the briars are thick with blackberries; and the chestnuts are fattening on the trees for a September fall. You could stock a larder with good things growing within the radius of a mile of the cottage.

Just down the hill there are wild boar being fattened up for a few smart restaurants that offer game on the menu. The deer are almost as common as sheep, and pheasants haunt the hedges and long grasses at the edge of fields.

In the honesty box next door there are five kinds of eggs to choose from, blue duck eggs, huge goose eggs, chicken, turkey and quail eggs. And displayed on a wooden table by his garden gate, our near neighbour Dick Rapson, the woodsman who has been cutting our lawn this lazy summer, offers his garden's best, courgettes, cabbage and pumpkin. And there is honey to be had from the old military man round the corner who keeps bees. At this time of the year, the five supermarkets in the town are almost redundant to the inventive cook.

Imagine the menu: roast pheasant with mushrooms and chestnut stuffing, new potatoes and buttered cabbage, followed by baked apples in pastry with a Victorian plum jam. And if last year you had the foresight to collect damsons, then you'd have a damson wine to go with your feast.

To be in England now that September is almost here with its autumn harvest is always a joy.

Chapter 10

Planting Myself 500 Years Into The Future

When you've lived on this earth for seventy years and received so much from it, I think of the food as just one aspect of being a guest at the banquet of the Earth's table, the wheat, the rice, the fruit, the vegetables, the meat, the cheese, the fish, the butter and the oils, the beans and pulses. The wine, the beer. There has been a great deal of taking and as much enjoyment. And the thought came to me that it would be good to give something back to the earth and the answer lay just to hand.

It has been a long hot summer here in England, this Coronavirus pandemic year of 2020, after an interminably long wet winter. The oak trees must have found conditions perfect because this autumn the crop of acorns is a record one. I've never seen the oaks carry such a freight of acorns, nor produce so many really big ones.

As I ride the woods near our home on my horse Callum, I constantly brush under oak branches laden with acorns standing proud in their cups and now and then I grab one or two choice samples, pale green and cream and put them in the pocket of my old Barbour wax jacket.

This week the rains came in earnest and the rock-hard

clay-like earth we have hereabouts is suddenly soft and yielding. The acorns in my pockets need planting now, and so I have obliged.

The horse paddocks on the farm where our small hamlet is nestled is short on trees for the horses to seek shelter under from the heat and the flies or to have something solid to rub against for a good scratch. So for all these reasons I put my acorn harvest into the now damp soil, at the very edge of the paddocks just beyond the fence posts, digging a small hole with a sharp stick and plugging each one with an acorn. My siting for each acorn should protect it from grazing horses while it is establishing itself. I push them in hard and cover them lightly with soil, hoping the energetic squirrels won't find them.

They should be fine, given the thousands of other acorns littering the forest floor and the footpaths around here. There is bounty enough for the squirrels. Pigs would have a field day and grow fat on the oak harvest this year.

As I plant each acorn, I make sure to be at least 50ft away from the last one; you don't want the new trees to be too close together. They need their own space, sunshine, and nutrients.

Walking up the hill slowly, stopping now and then to dig and plant, has a great satisfaction in it. I realise that if even only one or two of these giants makes it to maturity, I will have changed the landscape with a marker that could survive 500 years. It gives me pleasure to think that my handiwork will mark my brief passing with something as magnificent as an oak tree.

Each oak is home to so much life. Each part of the oak, roots, trunk branches and leaves is used to house everything from fungal spores to insects, to birds and squirrels and doubtless many other things I am not even aware of. It is like planting a city.

I like to think that some future courting couple or fly-pestered horse will find shelter under my oaks, those that escape the vagaries of the weather, the browsing of deer and horses and the farmer's flail. How good to think that something of me and my handiwork will survive when even the longest memory has forgotten my time on this earth. This little act of life-planting is for me as much as the tree.

I tell my wife and our son to keep an eye out in the future to see if any of the oaks survive. I am 70, my wife 60 and our son 30, so maybe our son may yet see the result of this autumn's planting, my acorn plucking from Callum's back now transformed into a stand of fine oaks, offering protection to many and a wind shield for the old cottage that has been our home for forty years here in England.

It is a good, if bittersweet, thought.

CHAPTER 11

ARMY RATIONS

If you love food as much as I do, you will find something to savour wherever you are, whatever your condition in life. My time in the South African Army doing my National Service was no exception, even though the pickings were thin.

I grew up with many of my father's favourite expressions and one that stayed with me is 'A good soldier learns to look out for himself and make himself comfortable'. This was quoted most often at one of our fishing lunches on the beaches or the rocks of the Cape, or at one of our picnic stops when driving long distances when a thermos flask of coffee and a cake tin of sandwiches and hard boiled eggs were produced.

It seemed most relevant and useful advice when I was a rookie rifleman at Oudtshoorn in 1969. It was quickly obvious that if you did not look out for yourself you would not eat well. The food was generally adequate, if completely unmemorable. So I asked my parents for some food parcels now and then and they did not disappoint. They sent four things: the South African staple, biltong (dried beef); buttermilk rusks for dunking in coffee; red apples; and four-pound slabs of fruitcake from my father's bakery. This addition to my diet was hugely welcome and an utter luxury. While I did share some, I was not as generous as I might have been.

One of the strange pleasures I came across in the army was the bully-beef sandwich. Now, like all foods, you want it when you are in the mood. Too much of a good thing palls. Which reminds me of a very beautiful girl I once courted. She dropped me for a friend of mine and I was not a little put out. But after a year of observing this relationship, I asked my friend how he felt about her. His answer is one I have never forgotten. 'Jules,' he said. 'Imagine living in a chocolate factory. After a while you get sick of chocolate.' And, doubtless, so too with bully beef sandwiches. But when you are hungry and come in from the heat of the shooting range, or you've been marching or running your butt off all day, then, after a good shower and clean overalls, a bully-beef sandwich is just what the doctor ordered. There are qualifications to this statement. The bread has to be white and just baked fresh, the bully beef mashed, and a little butter on the bread. And as your teeth sink into that goodness, my oh my, it's good.

So let's take it down a notch further on the tinned food scale. Imagine a dense forest inhabited by wild elephants near Knysna in the Cape. You are on army manoeuvres and it's cold, it's wet, the trees are dripping and you are driving a big moustachioed major around who is tireless in his pursuit of platoons fighting their way through the mud. His behaviour is not gentlemanly; he may be an officer, but he is no gent. He behaves like an animal. He would win any contest for assholes. You pulled the short straw when you got the gig as his duty driver of the day. You are not a happy camper, to put it mildly. You've been shouted at and struck by his swagger stick across the knuckles, even as you fight for control of the Jeep's bucking wheels in the rise and plunge, rise and plunge, of the forest tracks slick with mud. But when it's finally over and you've cleaned up and made your bed next to the Jeep in a camouflage-tented garage in a dense wood, you strike gold. Curious as to what is stacked next to the Jeep under a green army canvas cover you find more than fifty cardboard boxes of tinned condensed milk, some of the boxes already open. The grin on your face says it all. Lying in your sleeping bag slurping thick gloopy delicious, sweet condensed milk, you feel your energy return in waves. And suddenly life is very good.

Back in camp in Outshoorn after the excitements of Knysna, you are once more into the monotony of parade ground drill, gun drill – breaking down an FN rifle and reassembling it in under thirty seconds. And shooting practice out on the range or in a twisting *donga* (ravine) with automated targets of gunmen popping up to seemingly shoot back at you. Jumping out of moving trucks to throw a cordon of soldiers round a building. And map reading and more map reading. All the fun of infantry life. And as the day wraps up and you jog down to the canteen, you join a queue and find at its head one of the chefs doling out hot doughnuts. Good Lord! Hot doughnuts. And Heaven does not seem that far away.

I had a friend on the outside of the camp, Linda, a girl I never met, but who acted as a guardian angel (See *A Fisherman in the Saddle* [Blkdog Publishing 2021] for the whole story). She would alert me to surprise forced route marches or an exercise in map reading, where we'd be dropped in the middle of the night miles and miles from the camp and told to be back in under three days. Then you had to find water and survive off the land. In one never-to-be-forgotten incident, we barbecued a tortoise. But thanks to Linda, on this occasion, I managed to get a huge slab of fruitcake into my rucksack. After two days without any food, our group or 'stick' of riflemen were surviving on muddy water and fruitcake, and not complaining. I've never been more popular. The fruitcake tasted of salvation.

One Friday night, I was trucked off to a Jewish family in the town for a Sabbath supper. It was both very familiar and utterly weird. I'd had to scramble to get myself scrubbed up and into best battle dress kit. I found myself dropped off in front of a corrugated iron-roofed bungalow set in a lawned garden. The house was brightly lit, and I was both drawn to the front door and overcome with shyness. My hosts must have been watching, for when I hesitated on the path to their front door, it suddenly swung open and they came out to greet me. The motherly woman kissed me and her short stout husband put a hand on my shoulder and they walked me inside. I remember taking my beret off as I entered the house which was filled with the most sublime cooking smells, roast chicken among them, and other things harder to name. My hostess handed me a beer and we went through to their dining room. The table was beautifully laid with silver on a damask cloth, shining glasses and a floral centrepiece. Two young children, a boy of around ten and a younger girl stood by their chairs and smiled at me.

My hostess then lit the candles and sang the Sabbath prayer over a goblet of wine. Before her lay a magnificent plaited *kitke* loaf of bread just like the one we would have had at my own family home for the Sabbath meal that night.

I was immensely moved. I felt like a wild animal escaped from the army camp and yet despite this, I had been invited into a sacred space and made to feel welcome, so utterly welcome, a guest of honour. I would have found it hard to speak had I been addressed just then. I was invited to sit down, and supper commenced with the most delicious chicken soup I can remember and that soft, cake-like bread.

More at ease now, we spoke of inconsequential things, and they told me about their life and asked of my family, how my time in the army was going, and my future plans. I answered as best I could while savouring the roast chicken, followed by a delicious fruit salad. I ate and sipped my beer and looked at the light of the candles and I knew that my hosts observed how moved I was to find myself there. When it came time to leave, I found for the first and probably the last time in my life that I could not for the life of me speak. I simply squeezed their hands, not ashamed of the tears that threatened to roll down my cheeks. I had been fed a wonderful meal, but I was filled with so much more.

CHAPTER 12

A BIRTHDAY ON JUPITER

Our son Dominic has always had an interest in boats and sailing. It started with canoes on Ardingly Reservoir close to our home in East Sussex and progressed to small sailing dinghies. Then the day came on which we drove him down to the Brighton Sailing Club in the Marina to see if he could get a deck job with one of the Sunday sailors taking part in the weekly race offshore. He was 15 at the time.

After a few weeks he found he had a regular gig on one of the pacier boats and enjoyed himself greatly. One morning I walked to the end of the harbour's western arm to observe the flotilla of yachts exit the Marina and saw Dom busy on the foredeck unfurling a spinnaker. As luck would have it, with his proud father watching, an unexpected gust of wind suddenly filled the huge sail and Dom was para-sailing way out over the water beyond the bow. I held my breath as he clung onto the sail which as suddenly as it had filled with wind, deflated, and Dom returned to the yacht's deck none the worse for his flying experience. This event did not daunt him in the least and he continued to sail with the Brighton Marina yachties.

And then motorbikes claimed his interest and he did

not sail for some years. But the taste for adventure was well established. He did a trip through India from south to north with friends on scrambler motor bikes, then a 1,000-mile solo bicycle ride down the West Coast of the US, and, once back in the UK, he led bike rides from London to Paris and from John O'Groats to Land's End.

When he was in his late twenties, he and I both started watching the new breed of yachting vlogs on YouTube – young couples who buy a boat and take off round the world – and his interest in yachting was rekindled. His girlfriend Stephanie, a chemical engineer and a keen skydiver, runner and cyclist and into any and all forms of adventure sport, was hooked too and within a couple of months they began to look for a yacht to buy, both as a home in the Brighton Marina and also to sail.

After six months of criss-crossing the country to look at boats, they eventually found a 37-foot sloop in Plymouth which to my absolute astonishment, they sailed back to Brighton. Wisely, I thought, they engaged an experienced yacht delivery captain to assist them, but after she nearly ran them aground once and they had a couple of other near misses, they opted to dispense with her services and sailed on alone, quite uneventfully as it happened. They found a permanent berth in Brighton Marina, renamed the boat *Jupiter* and moved on board.

As with all second-hand yachts, *Jupiter* needed work and over the next few months they brought her fully up to speed and started to learn her ways while sailing up and down the Sussex and Kent coasts and undertaking a variety of navigational and seamanship courses. I was immensely proud of them both, being rather chary of the sea myself; as I had grown up in Cape Town fishing its coasts, I knew only too well how fickle the sea could be and how dangerous.

We visited them now and then for a cup of tea and *Jupiter* looked increasingly seaworthy and also homely below. Then they invited Jan and me to celebrate my 69th birthday with a sail down the coast which we were delighted to accept. The day was a perfect sunny one, surprisingly warm for May with just enough wind to allow us to ghost along west towards Brighton pier. This was sailing as I liked it, peaceful with a chance to relax and get a tan.

Neither of us was expecting to be fed more than a sandwich and so were amazed to find the table in the cockpit laid with a Sunday lamb roast and all the trimmings and a delicious bottle of red wine to go with it. I was deeply touched as lamb roast is my favourite and I enjoyed the meal hugely. As I ate, savouring every morsel, I thought of all those many Sunday mornings when I had sat in the car reading the *Observer* while Dominic found his sea legs. This was a pay-off that was sweet in so many ways.

After lunch Dom and Steph turned *Jupiter* about and we headed back to her berth in the Marina. This, I thought, was a birthday that would stick in my memory.

As any yachtsman will tell you, the departure and arrival in port are the really tricky bit and so it was lovely to see how well Dom and Steph managed the manoeuvres needed as we edged our way back into the marina, no fuss, no bother, everything going like clockwork. It boded well, I thought, for the circumnavigation around the coast of Britain that they were planning, and which they duly completed that October having had some excitements on the way which only deepened their love of the sea and sailing.

Once we were safely tied up once more in *Jupiter's* berth Steph popped below to get us some tea. When she arrived back in the cockpit it was with a tea towel covered bowl. Grinning like a Cheshire Cat, she removed the covering to reveal a bowlful of golden glazed *koeksisters*, a kind of plaited, syrup-soaked crisp doughnut concoction that is a staple of South African cooking.

To say that I was overcome is to understate the case. I was amazed and my emotional levels went through the roof, and I was so deeply touched, I only just managed to stop myself weeping. Jan and I had fallen in love with Steph as much as our son had. The months in which we got to know her just deepened our feeling for this brave, wise, kind and loving English girl. So when she unveiled the *koeksisters* it just utterly got to me. When I had thanked her, I took a bite and it was as if the 6,000 miles between the land of my birth and England had closed. In some strange way, as I ate those koeksisters, the two countries of my life became one.

Steph had added her own touch in making the koeksisters, infusing the syrup with lemon and lemon peel to cut down on the sweetness, a trick that worked beautifully. I nibbled on these sweets and sipped my tea, deeply content, emotional and so happy. It was truly the sweetest of birthdays. Sometimes it's about the food, but sometimes it's as much about the cook and the open-hearted hospitality that lingers longest in the memory.

CHAPTER 13

OBRIGADO PORTUGAL

Once in a while, a country shows you its heart the moment you arrive. That is how it was with Portugal.

It was 1985 and we were on a six-month caravan exploration of Europe, five years after we had arrived on the continent from South Africa, working as journalists on the *Mid Sussex Times*. We had finally achieved permanent residence status in the UK and now wanted to look about this new continent we'd made home; we wanted to explore.

Our plan was to head south, towing Florence (the lady with the gas lamps), our second-hand caravan, behind a black Renault 18 Turbo as far and fast as possible, to escape a freezing English winter, so our destination was the Algarve in Portugal.

We had previously had some contact with Portuguese neighbours in South Africa, where they formed a distinct community. And I had also met them in the two countries to the north of South Africa's borders in Angola and Mozambique, Portuguese colonies for centuries. It had given me a taste for things Portuguese, but I could not say I was too familiar with their culture.

Now, after a three-day drive from winter-locked

England, with snow still settling on our old stone cottage in East Sussex, we had made it in easy day drives down through France and northern Spain and then on to Coimbra, a charming university town on a river in Portugal. The last part of this marathon road trip had been through the mountains dividing Portugal from Spain and the blue-gum tree forests spoke to us of the Cape, which we still thought of as home. They felt familiar.

We found a small, wooded campsite in Coimbra and parked the caravan, set up its awning and went and had a hot shower. Clean, fresh and feeling revived, we walked into the town and down to the river where the first lights of the evening were reflected in the water. The weather in February felt spring-like, and an easy stroll along the river brought us to an inviting looking riverside restaurant. The place was almost deserted, but we were made welcome and shown to a table in the window that overlooked the river, a bridge across it and beyond, the twinkling lights of the town on its hill.

We then made a discovery that was a huge comfort through our whole stay in Portugal. As Britain's oldest ally and with strong links between the two nations based on the port and wine trade, many Portuguese spoke very good English. Many had also spent time working in the UK and had surprisingly fond memories of the place.

So on this night, as with so many during our stay, we were able to ask for suggestions as to what we should eat and drink and a delicious meal followed shortly. A bottle of light red wine arrived and then the green soup known as Caldo Verde, made with potatoes, collard greens or kale, sliced smoked sausage and olive oil. It is a light soup but surprisingly filling, tasting of the green vegetable married to potato, healthy and wholesome and served with wonderful crusty bread. Later we learned that this soup is one of the country's iconic dishes alongside salt cod, *bacalao*, for which there are endless recipes – one for each day of the year, according to the Portuguese.

Our next course arrived in small black-and-white speckled stoneware tureens. Lifting the lids, we met the country's best-known surf and turf combo, Pork Alentejo, a mix of cubed pork with clams. It was delicious in a robust home-cooked style, the pork tender and the clams sweet, the sauce a mix of land and sea. By the time we had finished, we were in that wonderful lethargic state you reach after a deeply satisfying meal at the end of a long tiring day. Happy to be in Portugal.

We declined dessert but were brought two glasses of port and the ubiquitous small egg custard in puff pastry known as *Pastéis de Nata*. The owner said it was on the house and smiled a welcome to Portugal. We felt embraced and at home. Portugal never had a better ambassador. That restaurant owner fed so much more than our stomachs that night in February 1985. And the bill was surprising in its modesty after UK prices. Thanking our host for a delicious meal and the warm welcome, we strolled back along the river to Florence, she of the many lamps, our home on wheels for the next six months. The adventure had truly started.

After a good night's sleep, the next morning found us wandering over the river up into the old town where we discovered the heart of the place, a stunning food and flower market close to the University. It was our first experience of a European food market, and it did not disappoint. The colours of the fruit and veg glowed in the morning sunshine, red and yellow, gold and green. It looked like a banquet fit for gods. And amid the soft, delicious scents there was a sharp, harder note of freshly brewed coffee from a coffee and pastry shop by the flower stalls. Who could ask for more? A delicious breakfast followed of fantastic bread and butter and a quince jam known as *marmalade*, served with a strong white sheep's cheese and cup after cup of great coffee.

After some sightseeing at the University, which was founded in 1290, we returned to the market to buy a picnic lunch, something we would repeat over and over again on many days when we'd found a good food market on our travels through this new continent we now called home. It was and remains one of the best ways to enter the local culture and eat well too. We bought rolls, cheese, huge tomatoes, smoked sausage, fruit and a bottle of wine and counted the change, once again astonished by how cheap things were here.

After a few days in Coimbra we packed up and headed west and then south along the coast, realising on the way that the peaceable Portuguese turned into demons behind the wheels of their cars. But we arrived unscathed in Nazare. In this spectacularly sited fishing town north of Lisbon, we were offered sea urchins cooked in the coals of a fire by the man running the caravan camp site. We tried a morsel each; it was delicious, rich and intense. The only other residents of the site, an American couple, made pigs of themselves and got terribly sick. We were glad we'd only tasted. Decades later I watched one of my food heroes, the effortlessly cool chef Anthony Bourdain, who died too young and by his own hand. He was eating fresh sea urchins out of their shells with relish and delight at the French Laundry in California.

And more recently, at Brophy's Restaurant harbour side in Santa Barbara with my brother Herman and his wife Teri, we noted the great purple heaps of sea urchins brought in by trawlers that had been working the waters offshore around the Channel Islands. This prickly fragile harvest was destined for seafood markets in Japan the next day. But still I held back. Tripe and sea urchins are foods I've ducked. I'm not one of those with an appetite for everything – from the pig's tail to its snout – as some say. Or the Chinese appetite for everything which moves on the earth and below and above.

Our caravan trip next took us to Lisbon, which we loved, and Cascais nearby where we based ourselves, a place on the sea with a royal palace and monasteries on the green mountain behind it.

And so to goat, or kid, cabrito, as the Portuguese call it. Flame grilled on the barbecue, or baked in the oven. We ate this for the first time with Portuguese friends we'd met on our travels. Fernando, a retired casino boss, was fishing in a harbour the other side of Cascais when we met and we established an instant bond. He took us home to meet his Scottish wife Margaret and their children. That evening, we were their guests at a nearby restaurant that specialised in goat. If you love lamb, you will love kid, which is as tender and juicy but less fatty and sweeter. We ate with gusto and a friendship was forged over the sacrificial kid that lasted until Fernando died and beyond, some forty years later.

We finally reached the Algarve after a fortnight of meandering down the Portuguese coast just in time to see the almond blossom clothe the hillsides. We stood at the country's south-westernmost point, at the exploration school of Prince Henry the Navigator at Sagres, from where the route to India around the Cape – our former home – had been plotted. That was a strange feeling, to stand on solid earth looking out to sea and feeling the dream of the Portuguese to find their way round the world from this very place. We were, in a way, time travellers, returned to tell of the success of their ventures into Africa and beyond.

If our hearts and minds were engaged at Sagres, so too were our stomachs, all along the Algarve.

With food, I sometimes find simple is best, and when you add charcoal and flames, simple becomes sublime. Chicken peri-peri with ice cold Vinho Verde, Portugal's green, slightly fizzy wine, is one such example. Looking at the canary-yellow flesh of the chickens in markets and butcher shops, heads, necks and claws still in place, you could see that the animals were fat and healthy and had lived a free-range life, with corn to supplement their diet. And then some red is added to the skin when the magic of peri-peri is supplied, the chilli concoction so beloved by the Portuguese and brought by them to world cuisine.

On the Algarve, we passed barbecue chicken restaurants by the dozen with separate fires for the huge, fat grilled sardines. All you had to do was to claim a table and the meal arrived, no menus, no fuss, bread and wine or beer, grilled sardines, a mixed salad and then the great gold and brown flame-burnished bird, one or two per table, depending on the number of people and their appetite. More bread, more wine, some sizzling hot potato chips, and you have all you need.

I would nominate such a restaurant as the equal or superior to so many fancier places I've eaten. You tear the bird apart easily and mop up the juices with the fresh bread. This would be a meal I would happily have as my last supper on earth if ever it came to that, and I was capable of eating.

The combination of crisp, spicy skin and succulent flesh that shouts 'CHICKEN' is pretty damn hard to beat. Washed down with a cold beer, or more Vinho Verde, it is just the best. The Portuguese laid-backness adds to the pleasure, as does the setting, maybe a narrow crowded restaurant under an awning, the sea glinting in the distance or close by, with the very trawlers that, bobbing on the tide, had brought those bouncing, fresh slightly metallic-tasting silver blackened fish to your table. And if you can eat an egg pastry after that, you are more of a trencherman than me. Coffee does me fine.

Our love affair with Portugal, begun with our caravan trip, has lasted and grown over the years, and we have made many return visits. Two years ago, fed up with another interminable English winter, we bolted for the eastern Algarve, hired a car at Faro airport and then drove east, booking into an apartment in the heart of the small, unassuming town of Tavira. We ate fresh tuna and seafood in the March sunshine and slept it off on the unspoiled beaches. Each day we explored further afield and found a mediaeval castle commanding the coast and lagoon at Cacela Velha, an old Moorish fishing village that offers a glimpse into Portugal's history. There aren't many tourist amenities in the town apart from a few restaurants, but here you'll find the remains of an eighteenth-century fort with stunning sea views as well as a beautiful beach with sandbars that you can walk out to when the tide is low. And just beyond a mile further east, the hamlet of Fabrik. Sitting at a restaurant on the beach at Fabrik, we were served *cataplana*, the Algarve's version of *bouillabaisse*, a seafood stew that lives on in my mind as one of the best seafood dishes I've eaten, period. The place had a deck overlooking the beach and I sat with my bare feet against the sandy boards beneath our table. The sun and the thought of freezing England warmed the cockles of my heart as I sipped ice cold vinho verde until the meal arrived and then I was gone. Gone somewhere into gustatory heaven. Jan, who has sat opposite me for most meals of our forty-three years together, was a little taken aback. 'You enjoying that?' she asked as I inhaled the meal.

I ate as if at home, elbows on the tablecloth, breaking crab legs and pincers, sucking out prawn heads and tails, lingering over the lobster tail and tasting the clams, the black mussel and the three kinds of fish in the pimento coloured and flavoured broth. If truth be told, I wanted more, it was that good; stuffed as I was, I wanted more. I knew, as I ate, that this was a meal that topped the best French bouillabaisse I'd ever eaten, including one memorable meal on the Croisette in Cannes when I was 35 and on that caravan tour around Europe. The waiter smiled at me, looking at my plate, wiped clean with the last of the bread. 'It was good?' he asked needlessly. My own grin said it all. 'It was fantastic, please tell the chef it was just wonderful!' He said he would.

A few minutes later, he returned with a rum baba for me, and a crème brûlée for Jan, compliments of the chef. I scoffed my dessert, every last morsel. Then we drove back slowly to our beds and I slept the rest of the afternoon away in the deep, untroubled slumber of the satisfied glutton.

That evening, we walked down to our favourite riverside bar in Tavira and ordered the giant balloon glasses of local gin and tonic with ice and sun-kissed lemons, the first few sips setting us up for the evening as swallows dipped to drink the silk surface of the river.

Obrigado, Portugal!

Chapter 14

France - My Other Home

A strange feeling comes over me the moment I drive off the Eurostar train and my car wheels touch French soil – I feel in some inexplicable way that I am home again.

The first stop for fuel adds to that feeling with the sight and taste of fresh croissants, pains au chocolat and the array of food on display, so very different from Britain. This is a country that makes no bones about its love affair with food. It is a passion. One of the differences between the two countries emerges at dinner party tables. In England, it's considered bad form to comment on the food, a bit 'non-U'. In France, part of the pleasure of eating is about knowing where the food came from and how it was cooked. And the cook is complimented. The one country has a Calvinist attitude to pleasure on a plate, the other a very Cavalier one – robust enjoyment publicly expressed. It is remarkable to me that two countries divided by 20 miles of water can be so different.

Dining out in France can be intimidating. There is still a respect for formality and for knowledge when it comes to food. Your waiter will quickly have your measure the moment you open your mouth and speak English. He will not expect much of you after that. But if by chance you have a few words of '*simpatico*', you will improve your experience instantly.

By way of contrast, he will respect that middle-aged French couple who know their food and wine, who engage him in conversation about the restaurant's menu and ask his advice on what is good. His respect will grow when he hears which wine they choose to accompany the food. And he will be further impressed by the way they deal with the food and how they enjoy it. Their respect, understanding and enjoyment of the food enhances his own standing as a part of the machine that delivers such pleasure. This attitude to food, the opposite of grab a bite and go, is one of the things that sets France apart from the English-speaking world.

One of the best arguments a foodie can mount for France is evident in every *boulangerie* window display. The glazed apple, pear, strawberry, peach, and apricot tarts, the coffee or chocolate iced *choux* pastry buns filled with cream, the coconut confections, the choice seems endless and all of it is delicious. The wicker baskets of baguettes and loaves of arresting size and shapes, the gleaming heaps of croissants. Where do you start? A visit to any kind of food store, a butchery or a delicatessen or a supermarket will dazzle you with beautiful hams, and sausages, pâtes, and ready to go meals. Prepare to eat well in France. Admittedly, these days, it might take a little more homework than fifty years ago, but there is still great food to be found.

The store cupboard of my memory is chock full of meals eaten in France that made me glad to be alive. My 35th birthday was a case in point. It was 1985 and Jan and I were on our caravan tour of Europe. We found ourselves in Cannes during May, the time of the Film Festival. We parked Florence in a campsite set in a cherry orchard in full fruit. You could lean out of the window and pick deep black-red cherries the size of plums that had that wonderful tang, both sweet and acidic, with a slightly metallic aftertaste. We looked around to see if we could spot any film stars, but saw none in our walks around the town.

For us, the star of Cannes was its truly spectacular food markets. If Heaven looks something like this, I would be content to be consigned there, I thought. We homed in on the covered arcaded market known as Marche Forville in the old town near the Croisette and the harbour. Being on the coast, this market had a lot of seafood fresh from the Mediterranean – shrimp, clams, scallops and *dorade* (sea bream) among other fish and shellfish. There were several vendors offering a delicious variety of cheeses, both local and from around the country. And there were cascades, Niagras, of fruit and vegetables of every kind and some I'd never met previously. There were ready-to-eat dishes such as paella, fried squash blossoms and tapenades, pizza and chickens on the spit. There was every kind of preserved meat, hams, salamis, wild boar sausages. We found a stall that offered ready-made meals with duck and selected two portions of duck in fresh cherry sauce for my birthday lunch. We walked back to the caravan, our bags groaning with pâte, cheese, wine, fruit and flans, plus the duck dish. We laid it out under the awning and set to. It was a meal to savour, and the centrepiece, the salty, rich, unctuous duck, with its browned skin and melting flesh, in the palate-cleansing cherry sauce. With, it we drank a crisp rosé whose name escapes me. It was one of the best birthday meals of my life; a feast in the most perfect setting in France.

A few days later, we lunched on the Croisette in Cannes, by the old harbour, and made another life-changing discovery, *bouillabaisse* with garlic toast, *rouille* and grated Gruyère cheese. The yellow-red, olive oil infused fish stew is a picture even before you experience the enjoyment of eating it.

We had picked a place to eat randomly and knew enough to order the *bouillabaisse.* The depth of flavour in this soup stew was mind-blowing, the seafood hiding below the orange sunset depth, sweet and delicious, and the first taste of the garlic mayonnaise *rouille* on garlic toast sprinkled with the Gruyère just demanded another and another mouthful. It is a one-dish wonder and eaten in the sunshine in Cannes beside the Mediterranean, it is hard to beat. If you are seriously into food, this dish is a big one to tick off, rather like the first time a twitcher, a bird-watching fanatic, sees a bald eagle. It's a prize for sure.

A few weeks earlier, on this journey around France, we had stopped in Sète, on the French Mediterranean coast just north of the Spanish border. It sits on one of the only hills on this coast and its business is that of a fishing port. There are lagoons in the area which attract wind surfers, yachties and thousands of wild birds. But we headed into the old part of town and found ourselves in a comfortable old hotel, quite formal in its way with high domed ceilings in the dining room, which at noon was crowded with a well-upholstered clientele. It all boded well, and we were not disappointed. We had a goat salad starter which was pretty good, and then our main course arrived: *moules farcies*, crumbed stuffed mussels on the shell, and this dish was a revelation. It was one of those dining moments when you know you've hit the jackpot. We'd noticed other diners ordering this dish made up of concentric circles of black mussels, their fat orange flesh coated in herbed crumbs using a parsley pesto. The waiter approved and we ate like gods. The crisp, fried crumb coating, the meltingly tender fresh mussels offset by the herby parsley was a fabulous combination, one to rival that of the more commonly found moules Marinière. It is moments like this when you taste France, when you profoundly understand in your very gut that you are the recipient and the beneficiary of a truly great food tradition with a massively sophisticated palate and a respect for food second to none. 'Stuffed mussels in Sète on the Mediterranean coast' are words that ring down the years as one of my memorable eating experiences. To make something so sublime from such simple local ingredients, mussels, parsley and crumbs, that is the French genius at work. And as you eat you know that there is no place in England where you might have had a lunch like this in an old, comfortable, middle-class, bourgeois hotel restaurant out in the provinces.

Many years later, as new parents of our son Dominic, we decided on a first holiday en famille and headed down the French Atlantic coast to Gascony, land of duck dishes and prunes, and found ourselves tucked into a pretty gîte on a traditional working farm. Jan fed and bathed Dom and put him down to sleep, tired after a long day's drive from England. She switched on the baby monitor that would alert us to his cries if he woke in this strange new place and then we walked across the courtyard to the main house and into a time warp.

Our hostess was an old peasant woman whose kitchen-cum-dining room boasted beams, hung with copper pots and a huge open fire range. It was like escaping the present and finding yourself dining in the seventeenth century. She spoke not a word of English and there was no menu. She served us glasses of Floc de Gascogne, the local tipple, a magical mix of local apple brandy Armagnac and grape juice, rich in raspberry aromas and red fruits. A glass of this ambrosia set our appetites racing.

Madame sat perched on a low stool by the fire in an old rusty black dress and a floral apron, and with the most basic of implements served up a meal I will never forget. Our expectations of excellence were not high and so the surprise was all the greater. First came plates of a robust home-made coarse pâte with a bitter herb salad and fresh baguette slices. The pâte had pistachio nuts in it and chunks of herby meat amid the liver binding. It was delicious and the bitter herb salad helped to clear the palate. With it we drank a bold deep black-red wine. And as we ate, Madame worked on two huge duck breasts that later we would learn were called Magrets de Canard. A speciality of south-west France, the magret is the breast of a duck or goose that has been fattened for foie gras and is one of France's favourite dishes. Coated with a thick layer of fat, it has the meatiness of steak, but a deeper character reminiscent of game. By the time it came off the grid above the wood coals, the fat rendered down to a delicious crispness and the meat still pink, it was served with dauphinoise potatoes, both crisp and creamy. Our glasses were refilled with the robust wine from a bottle that bore no label.

So often when one is served something delicious there is just not enough of it, and one eats, hankering for more. Not so on this occasion. There was enough for four people. The old lady smiled with satisfaction, seeing our delight. Jan, who speaks reasonably good French, thanked her again and again. And the baby monitor stayed silent.

To end this spectacular meal, we were served thick wedges of apricot *tarte tatin*, upside down apricot flan, just warm, with great dollops of clotted cream. Coffee and glasses of Armagnac finished the meal and nearly finished us. I would hate to know the calorie count of that meal, but we were young and hungry and never thought of such things in those days. We were intensely happy and delighted with this unexpected discovery in the deepest part of the country, *la France profonde.*

In the days that followed that memorable meal, we did day trips with the car, discovering the countryside and picnicking by the roadside in fields and vineyards and apple and plum orchards. The day would start with coffee in great mugs with fresh baguette slices, butter and five kinds of homemade jam, then it would be off to find a food market for the makings of a picnic lunch. These never disappointed and we came away with pâtes and cheese, or a serving of seafood paella, or a hot chicken off the rôtisserie, or slabs of anchovy, tomato and cheese pizza, great twisted heritage tomatoes, plums and apricots, or bunches of grapes and one or two small glazed fruit tarts. After lunch all three of us would have a doze and later in the apple, smoke and herb scented dusk we would wind our way slowly back to the farmhouse for another culinary treat. We were literally eating France.

Now and then, to change the routine, we would skip breakfast at the gîte, buy croissants at the boulangerie in the local village and eat in a café where much would be made of Dominic. It was heart-lifting to walk into shops and be greeted with the cheerful '*Bonjour Madame, Monsieur*' and '*Bonne journée*' on our departure. These small interactions before and after selecting our choices from the groaning stacks of bread and rolls just got the day off to a great start. Golden days of our youth.

In the years ahead, we would holiday on the Côte D'Azur near Cavalaire, west of St Tropez, and enjoy the swimming, the food and the bastide villages. These included one or two with shops specialising in jewellery made from trade beads sent from Venice into Africa for centuries, now restrung and reset for sale to tourists on the French Riviera. I felt a certain kinship with these objects, produced in Europe as my DNA was, and then some centuries in Africa, and now once more back in Europe.

Because of the easy access to the French Atlantic coast from our home in East Sussex, we often found ourselves over the years in Normandy, Brittany, in La Rochelle, and further south in Bayonne and Biarritz. And on these trips, invariably we would taste the seafood so richly and abundantly available here in the many cafés, bistros and restaurants.

The beautiful artists' hideaway of Honfleur in Normandy stole our hearts early on with its charming mediaeval streets, its double inner and outer harbour, and its sailor church with the roof of an upturned boat, and the street upon street of seafood restaurants. Sitting under a sun-dappled, butter yellow awning outside one such restaurant, we had no need to see the menu. Each table of busy French diners was grappling with a half-cartwheel size triple decker stand of *fruits de mer*, crayfish, prawns, crabs, black mussels, white mussels, cockles, winkles, sea urchins and other lesser-known shellfish molluscs. The scene could have been and indeed was painted by many French and British artists. The place was en fête with seafood-eating holidaymakers. This was life and it was for living and that meant eating. We tucked in ourselves, cautiously at first and then, appetites whetted, with abandon.

In our drives down this coast, we would on occasion lunch at a motorway petrol station and be astonished by the food on offer. One dish that became a loved staple of travel was hot smoked ham with potato salad. Plates heaped generously and with a beer to hand, we would tuck in, our destination and the journey ahead forgotten in the moment of food pleasure.

Further south, Brittany is a world unto itself and in its way reminds us of the rockbound coasts of our birthplace. As in the South African Cape, the tides are tremendous and dangerous, but the scenery spectacular, with its great beaches, the hidden coves, the inland waterways and seas. There is space to find solitude and when hungry there is a huge variety of the local speciality to choose from – buckwheat crêpes.

These come filled with cheesy seafood or with jam or ham or virtually anything you care to name including chocolate. Our kids loved this pancake paradise. This is where Dominic had his first real taste of yachting in the warm under a blue sky, and he never forgot it.

Let's leave France for now at La Rochelle, that most

gracious of seaports on the French Atlantic littoral. I was in favour of the place well before I ever saw it, because my mother had attended a school in Paarl, South Africa, named La Rochelle by French Huguenot descendants in the Cape. La Rochelle is in the Charente-Maritime department, near the wild, stormy Bay of Biscay. The Huguenots rebelled there in 1627 and 1628; no wonder I feel at home here. The Huguenot blood of the Bassons runs in my veins.

For centuries, the towers of La Rochelle have stood sentinel over the Old Port, one of France's most important sea outlets from the fourteenth to the seventeenth centuries. It was the point of departure for the New World by adventurers like the founders of Montreal, Canada. The arcaded streets and half-timbered houses of the old town remain from those mediaeval times, complemented by extensive parks and fine local beaches.

Le Phare du Bout du Monde (the lighthouse at the end of the world) in the bay facing La Rochelle is a replica of the one near Cape Horn. The marina of La Rochelle boasts 4,800 moorings and now ranks among the largest marinas in the world. No doubt as Dom and Steph sail about the world ,they will put into La Rochelle one day and a huge 300-year-old circle will have closed. Out of France by ship to Africa and back from Africa into France once more, over some ten generations.

Usually, when choosing a restaurant in a new city, I will follow my nose, my instincts and the locals. But on our first trip to La Rochelle, I did some research and we found the restaurant, which was rammed. After a short wait during which we strolled along the harbour wall, we were seated. I ordered a white Burgundy, an onion soup starter followed by creamy sole, and butter fried scallops. The soup was almost solid with caramelised onions and a round of toasted bread sinking beneath Gruyere cheese. You could stand a spoon up in it. It was for me the definition of what an onion soup should be, sweet and savoury in one. And the fish course, with its combination of the morning catch, was perfection, the wine sublime. Thinking of that other great fish meal in Portugal, I ended with another rum baba. Holy mother, that was good.

France takes some beating. I've not met its match in this life. One of the many pleasures it has offered is the joy our children found there, for so many reasons within its food offering and well beyond. They would ponder the dessert menu, carefully weighing up the ice cream flavours on offer, make their choice and confirm to the waiter that yes indeed they wanted four scoops, *quatre balles* in French, or as the low Roup sense of humour has it, 'Cat's Balls'.

For me and my family, France is decidedly, eminently, unapproachably, the very definition of the Cat's Balls.

Vive La France!

CHAPTER 15

MEMORABLE MEALS

There are restaurants that live on in the memory as simply the best of their kind. Mostly it's because of the food, sometimes the setting, now and then the ambience. These are places that include the long gone as well as those that are still in business.

There is nothing more fickle than an eating-place. It just needs a new chef or new owners for its excellence to vanish overnight, and the treat you were expecting turns into ashes in your mouth. That said, I have been fortunate to know one or two that were spectacular for years and one or two are still in business.

Growing up in Cape Town, I was spoiled for choice, there were many fine places to eat, but my all-time favourite was a steakhouse in Rondebosch, now long gone, called Barbeque. It was on the main road just below the gardens of the President's home, Groote Schuur. It had a cowboy feel of rough wood and its name was burned into a length of plank. You entered, I seem to recall, through the kind of bat's wing swing doors you get in a cowboy saloon. The place competed with The Hussar just across the traffic lights which was pretty damn good too, and Nelson's Eye in the City centre. If you wanted steak this was the place, ribs and lamb chops too.

The steak was the best I've ever eaten anywhere in the world, by a country mile. Back in the 1970s I was too uptight and shy to ask how they achieved such perfection, I just enjoyed it. I used to order the sirloin, which was cut thick, a good inch, maybe more and obviously aged. It was also marinaded in some dark concoction which left a glaze on the meat, and it was cooked over wood coals on an open grill fire. Served medium-rare for me, it came on a wooden plank with fabulous chips, breaded onion rings, a salad, or a fruit salad, or both. And it would take a good half an hour to eat. It was and remains the finest beef I've ever eaten, and if I could, I would book a table now and eat there one more time. In a heartbeat.

The place has stayed on in my imagination as a cave of treasure, a room of wonders, eating at its very best. I would get there, usually at the weekend after a day in the saddle, having ridden down to the False Bay coast and now with an appetite to do justice to the meal. With it, I drank the local Castle Lager beer which was pretty good too. Those steaks set a benchmark which have never been topped, not in France not in the USA, they were phenomenal.

If you love fish, you will love Cape Town. It offers some of the best in the world. Yellowtail is my favourite, this white, meaty fighting fish has a taste and a texture all its own, maybe slightly metallic. Cooked in butter and lemon or grilled, it is a stunning offering from the sea. In the Cape, you have a fantastic selection to choose from: tuna, kingklip, snoek, kabeljou, grunter, red roman, hake, blacktail, mussel cracker steenbras, calamari, crayfish and prawns and many other varieties too, with as many ways to cook them as a 300-year heritage will provide.

There was a place which lives on in my mind that would put most of that seafood on your plate in a completely artless, unpretentious way, as if such excellence and abundance was no big deal, and at a knockdown price, if you were visiting from abroad. At Orca in Melkbosstrand up the west coast, some 20 miles from Cape Town you were as welcome in a bathing costume and flip flops straight from the beach or dressed up for the meal, be it lunch or dinner. At Orca, I ate some of the freshest and most beautifully prepared fish and shellfish that I have ever tasted. Strangely enough, it was also served on a wooden board. Just a hundred yards from the white sandy beach, it was a down-home sort of place with a great buzz.

Their seafood platter was enough for two and you and your partner would struggle to finish it. On the serving board there would be the catch of the day, plus mussels, calamari, some prawns and a crayfish tail. And all of it for a price that foreign visitors just could not believe. If I had to choose between Orca's best and a French triple platter of *fruits de mer,* it's no contest: for me, Orca wins, hands down.

It's an elbows-on-the-table kind of place, where nobody will turn a hair if you wipe your mouth with the back of your hand if your fingers are clutching crab, crayfish or prawns. The first thing I do there after finding a table is to kick off my shoes. Afterwards, a walk on the beach is a great way to end your lunch or supper. If you are very brave, you might even risk a swim in the icy sea, feeling your shoulder muscles contract with the shock. And if you are really lucky, you may even spot a whale or an Orca offshore.

In my time in Cape Town, before I left for my forty years in Europe, I was dating, looking for 'the one', and my favourite date idea would be a dinner and then maybe to go dancing. One of the most elegant places I've eaten at was an old Cape Dutch farmhouse named Kronendal on the road from Constantia Nek to Hout Bay. Its setting was within two ranges of mountain, giving it a Tinus de Jongh painterly feel, and its steep thatched roof, whitewashed walls and green shutters offered a sophisticated country welcome. Within, it was all old chandeliers, polished floorboards, oil paintings and crisp white table cloths bedecked with local flowers and candlelight offering a private glow. The waiters, in black with white knee length aprons, could have been from a Parisian restaurant. The food was as elegant as its setting. And the place oozed romance. If memory serves me right, there was a pianist in the corner tinkling the ivories and classical music on the soundtrack when he was sipping a drink at the bar during his break. In my twenties, I thought of this place as a treat and as pretty much perfect. Looking back with hindsight fifty years on, I wasn't wrong, it had put all the ingredients together and created something pretty special. And the food matched the ambience. It was the first time I suppose that I had met something approaching *haut cuisine*, where subtle flavours met and made beauty on the plate. The place cast such a spell that my date and I would often end up talking late into the night, all thought of dancing forgotten.

As a South African, I've eaten my fair share of 'braais' as barbecues are known in the land of my birth. And generally they are pretty good too. More unusual is the fish barbecue and without a doubt the best I've ever eaten was at the open-air beachside eatery known as Muisbosskerm, north-west of Cape Town, near Lamberts Bay.

Muisbosskerm derived its name from a shelter being built from a bush called 'Muisbos' by the long-gone native herdsmen, who migrated up and down this coast during the different seasons to pasture and water their sheep herds. The brainchild of Edward & Elmien Turner, Muisbosskerm was situated right on the shore, 5km south of Lambert's Bay on the Elands Bay Road.

This seemingly simple place offered barbecued crayfish with butter lemon and garlic and a wide variety of fish, baked, smoked and grilled, as well as the traditional 'waterblommetjie' and 'hotnotskool' stew, and fresh homemade bread straight from the clay-oven, with farm butter and the region's famous grape jam made from the wonderfully sweet and slightly scented Hanepoort desert grape. A plate of hot smoked snoek with this jam is the stuff of foodie dreams. These are just a few of the dishes to choose from in this self-help buffet meal.

To sit just back from the crashing waves, with your feet in the sand, eating world class seafood under the warmth of the southern sky surrounded by sand dunes and overturned clinker-built fishing boats, was a one-off culinary experience not easily forgotten.

And then there are three meals that encompass the best of Italy. We were on our 1985 caravan trip and found ourselves parked up in the mini-mediaeval Manhattan of San Gimignano in Tuscany, northern Italy. The fourteen old stone towers and the Tuscan Hills were as beautiful as our reading had promised. This small walled mediaeval hill town repaid hours of wandering around in its atmospheric setting.

Originally an Etruscan village, the settlement was named after the bishop of Modena, San Gimignano, who is said to have saved the city from Attila the Hun in 450.

The strange stone skyscrapers were all about neighbourly competition, building a tower taller than the neighbours. Originally seventy-two in number, they became a popular way for prominent families to flaunt their power and wealth. In 1348, plague wiped out much of the population and weakened the local economy, leading to the town's submission to Florence in 1353.

Here the past feels present, but this being Italy, it comes with vitality and brio. One evening we drove into Siena for a meal and found ourselves in the central piazza, Piazza del Campo, where that crazy mediaeval-style horse race, the Palio di Siena, takes place annually. We found a table at a restaurant in the square and as we sat down, a full moon rose about the ancient city walls, casting the beautiful architecture into bold relief. The gentle wash of an Italian evening was all about us, children playing in the square, a dog or two on their explorations and couples strolling in the dusk. Few seemed aware that this fabled setting was a UNESCO World Heritage site.

We ate a number of delicious things, including delicate salami and a salad tricolore, followed by a local speciality that I had not eaten until then, the pine nut and basil paste known as pesto on al dente spaghetti with a dusting of parmesan cheese. We drank a light red wine with it. The meal's seeming simplicity and its perfect execution live on in the mind. It was sublime. And in that ancient setting I felt a privilege and a gladness to be alive.

As we ate, in my mind's eye a parade of Etruscans passed by, then Roman legions, Hannibal and his elephants recovering from their crossing of the Alps, the Huns, the armies of the Germans and the Allies. The very stones of the piazza must be bathed in blood, sweat and tears, not all of it from the horses and their jockeys who stampede around it annually.

Later on this trip, we would walk the crowded squares, lanes and bridges of Venice and take the obligatory gondola boat ride. We shopped for leather and Jan came away with a beautiful suede suit of a delicate pale blue. Venice did not disappoint; how could it? The place is everything and more than you are led to expect, despite the crowds. It is a jewel box thrown open across a lagoon, its skyline unique and heart-achingly beautiful, and you see it twice, once on land and once reflected in its waters.

One night after the crowds had dispersed, we walked deep into the city's stone and water maze and found ourselves seated at a waterside restaurant eating whitebait *frito misto*, a mix of lightly battered crisp fresh anchovies and tiny calamari, sipping a crisp chilled white wine from the hills beyond the lagoon. It was thrilling to be there, and the food and wine were the perfect accompaniment.

And then we did it all again, but this time at lunch in Desenzano on Lake Garda – the *frittura di Paranza,* a simple fry- up of assorted small fish, squid, and prawns, eaten with a generous squeeze of lemon, was just as good and the animated setting of that harbour square just off the lake, accessed by a low humpbacked bridge, was just magical. The charm of being in Italy was borne in on us by smiling, flirty waiters, fish-tailed castle wall crenulations echoed in the split tails of squeaking swifts above milky turquoise water. Heaven would be hard pressed to beat that setting.

Let me finish with a meal that included all the elements I love, the outdoors, horses, fish and food – eating Japanese tempura, deep fried battered prawns and vegetables, at Burghley Horse Trials on a sunny summer day.

This was the happy setting for my introduction to tempura, served from a humble catering van and eaten as we watched the dressage phase of the event against the grand setting of Burghley House. I could not believe the lightness and crispness of the tempura batter which utterly transformed the eating quality of the courgette, aubergine, broccoli and onion. I seem to recall Jan and I sharing a return visit to the van out of embarrassed greed.

These are just some of the meals that live on in my memory, which is no longer the best. But these I remember well and the enjoyment lives on.

Chapter 16

Food for Falling in Love

Falling in love has the power to invest the most humble ingredients with passion and the minutest and most articulated memory of pleasure.

I met Jan again at Rhodes University, but now she was not the kid from the stables where I used to ride, but a lovely 18-year-old first year student, with a disarming honesty, directness and stunning copper-coloured hair in a gamine cut. We discovered that we were both there to do a Bachelor of Journalism degree. I was 27 and there as a mature student trying to build my life on something more stable and academic than a matric and some years as a biscuit salesman for my father's bakery.

We met at a University dance for first years and it was all awkwardness. But I had offered to give her and a friend a lift to the river estuary where I was rowing with the Varsity eight the next day, as she was keen to get out of her girls' residence for some sea and sun. I never thought she would actually show up at the appointed time of seven the next morning, but there she was outside her hall of residence, waiting for me and holding a beach bag. Her friend could not make it, she said, and so the two of us drove down to Port Alfred where my team, for whom I rowed bow, got thoroughly thrashed in our race. One or two of them were rowing later in the day in singles or pairs so I felt obliged to stay on to see how they fared.

And so I faced a day of chatting to Jan while I waited for these other races. It was a conversation that changed my life and 43 years later it is still ongoing. I quickly discovered that she was better read than me in English and that she also spoke French and had read widely in that language too, which I neither spoke nor read. She was the owner of some strong political opinions which I shared and in many ways was much older than her years.

Like me, she was the product of a rocky family life, and it was this I think that created the first deep bond between us, our dysfunctional families. She got me, despite the fact that I was nine years her senior. By the time the sun was lowering in the sky behind us I was more than intrigued by her and no longer felt lonely in my new life at Rhodes.

On the 20-mile drive back to Grahamstown I asked her out to supper so that we might continue our conversation. I dropped her off at her residence to shower and change and collected her an hour later for a meal at the local Chinese, a very small and modest place with a limited menu. I did not know it then, but she had needed to make her apologies to another student who had previously asked her out for that evening. But our visit to the sunny coast of Port Alfred had done for him.

I cannot remember a thing about that meal. It was Jan who had my undivided attention. By the time I got to bed that night I was in love with someone I knew could be a future life partner. I found her remarkable and intriguing and more than my equal in many ways, despite the age gap. She had a quiet strength and determination that I respected. As a friend would say about finding someone special, I had found the other half of the orange.

And now food entered the picture. Jan said that the food at her hall of residence was not exactly memorable and so I began to cook for us at my flat and we used to enjoy going to Grey's Dam just outside of town, where we would swim and canoe and for lunch, I would make an almost instant barbecue with dried wood collected from the waterside. From my flat I would bring a salad or maybe just a couple of tomatoes, salt and pepper, some buttered bread rolls and four or six lamb chops. We would eat with our hands, straight off the wire barbecue grill that the meat was cooked on, and then swim again. The smell of the lamb cooking, the wood smoke and our sunscreen oil made a scent that can still take me back to that time. For a while, we could put thoughts of our journalism degree to one side, glad to be out of the Reserve Library where we seemed to spend most of our days and evenings.

Rhodes University was 700 miles from Cape Town, a drive of some eleven hours that we did regularly for the university holidays. It was a very long day behind the wheel of my small yellow Datsun. We shared the driving, and it would fly by with Jan reading to me tirelessly. I recall Roald Dahl featuring a couple of times. Before leaving we would make a flask of coffee for the journey and sandwiches with crisp bacon and peanut butter, a filling to which we became addicted. A few apples or some oranges and the catering for the journey would be done. Having food with us cut down on the time of the journey, as we only had to stop once for fuel. I remember those drives with fondness and the sandwiches with great pleasure, the fresh squidgy bread, the salty bacon and the sweet nutty peanut butter.

Sometimes I would drive the last mile to Jan's family home not quite sure how we'd got there, as my mind had been held by the world of the book she was reading to me or by our conversation, and the driving was on autopilot, I knew the road so well.

And so three years flew by. One of the highlights of the university week would be Jan waking me up on Sunday mornings. She would walk the mile from her hall of residence to my flat, stopping on the way at Paula's Bakery for warm Copenhagens which we ate with coffee in bed, savouring being together in the Sunday morning quiet.

And then there was the final drive home to Cape Town and three weeks to organise our wedding amid the mayhem of preparing to emigrate to the UK after a skiing honeymoon in Austria.

Our wedding in Cape Town at the end of our third

and final year took place in the garden of the Alphen Hotel in Constantia. It was a perfect Cape summer's day and Jan looked ravishing in her sleeveless cream Greek inspired dress, holding a simple bouquet put together for her by her bridesmaid Fiona Powrie. I remember a sense of deep happiness and of gratitude, aware of my debt to Jan for being a huge help in getting me through my degree. After the speeches we circulated among the guests, knowing we would not be seeing them for a long time, as we would be moving abroad very shortly. By the time we were hungry, all the food had been served and there was nothing of the wedding feast left for us.

Jan's mother Lynne urged us to take our leave as she said no one would feel free to go until we had gone, and so Jan changed into her going away dress and we said our farewells, even though we would have much preferred dancing late into the night.

We drove up to my parents' home nearby, which stood dark and silent, and raided the fridge. I remember sitting on the deck looking out at the twinkling lights of the suburbs below Bishopscourt as we ate our first meal as husband and wife. Once more, I forget what we ate, it was not important. We may have missed out on the wedding meal, but it did not matter in the least.

Then we drove back to the Alphen Hotel, where we had a room booked for the first night of our honeymoon. Soon we would be leaving the Cape for England and I knew that with Jan by my side a great adventure was beginning, and I felt no fear of the future, just joy.

Chapter 17

Spain on a Plate

There is something savage about Spain, which gives it an edge that adds to the pleasure of travel there. I'm not talking of the hybrid tourist Spain of the Costas, the hangout of partying British youth, elderly retired Brits and British criminals. I'm talking of Spain itself.

You feel watched, observed, and there is a certain formality, yet once this is broached there is an immense warmth. But, that said, the ruling spirit here is still busy digesting the civil war and its dead. Far from driving over lemons, here you could well be driving over graves.

No two people ever visit the same country and no two people read the same book. Each country is a kaleidoscope of images, partly selected and constructed by your own history, reading, study, feelings and views. The Spain I visited first in 1970 was a country cocktail made up for me by Hemingway, Laurie Lee, Picasso's *Guernica*, El Greco, Velasquez, the Moors, the Jews, the expulsion of the Jews by King Ferdinand and Queen Isabella in 1492 and Franco and his patent leather capped Guardia Civil, Spanish dance and bullfighting. A very strange cocktail with a bitter aftertaste.

I knew next to nothing of the country myself; it was all second-hand impressions. And of course that was the country

I found, alongside a far more pedestrian version, of food markets and flea markets and antique markets. The first thing I bought in Spain was a pair of rawhide leather cowboy boots which were incredibly stiff at first and then, as they moulded to my feet, incredibly comfortable and almost indestructible. I wore them for years for horse riding and casual wear, and literally wore them to death.

The Spain I first met in 1970 was Madrid, on the first and only family holiday in Europe of the kind that took in the major capitals. I remember a rooftop swimming pool at our hotel, horse-drawn carriages in the huge city parks, the strange street furniture, the posters for bullfights, the outdoor cafes, the formality and the strolling pairs of ominous looking police in those ridiculous patent leather kepis. It was June, so high summer and, aged 20, I picked up on a voluptuousness in the air, and the attractiveness of the young women. And a watchfulness that I did not comprehend.

In 1985, I returned to Spain with Jan on our extended caravan journey. of Spain and Europe. Having a partly Jewish heritage, I was acutely aware of the history of the Jews in Spain, their lives under the Moors, and later, the increasing attacks suffered under the resurgent Christian Spain.

In the very month of July 1492 that Ferdinand and Isabella gave Christopher Columbus his order to set sail for the discovery of the Indies, they published the edict that all Jews (some 200,000) who had not converted to Catholicism should be driven out of their kingdom. So Jewish history and the discovery of the Americas are linked in Spain. Even as Columbus sailed west, other Spanish sea captains filled their ships with Jews for exorbitant passage prices and then dumped them at sea. Tens of thousands died trying to flee Spain. Many were murdered by brigands, hoping to find diamonds and gold coins in Jewish stomachs, a story spread by deadly rumours.

The expulsion was the pet project of the priest Torquemada who headed the Inquisition. The belief was that if Jews were allowed to stay, they would influence the recent converts to return to their Jewish faith. The surviving Jews spread out across the Mediterranean countries. and many found sanctuary in Turkey.

So as I walked around Spain it was with feelings not dissimilar to those I feel when I visit Germany. And yet, and yet, I have had and continue to have a love for Spain, born out of its culture and its food and its literature. What writer has not at some stage found themselves tilting at windmills? I have just completed such a book, *Life in a Time of Plague* (Blkdog Publising, 2020), the windmill in this case being the wildly flailing arms of Boris Johnson and his pitiful government, which has the blood of thousands of Britons on its hands.

And so we found ourselves in Spain in February 1985, on a cold winter's night in a deserted campsite somewhere near the city of Salamanca, with dust-devils driven by a freezing wind on a vast, flat plain. It was not an auspicious start, and the next day we made it across the mountains into Portugal. A few months later we crossed the Guadiana River from Portugal's Algarve coast back into Spain and headed for Jerez and Cadiz. Immediately, we found excellent bread, olive oil, tomatoes, fruit and vegetables, superior to that we'd had on the Algarve. If I had to find words to sum up what Spanish food means to me, it is all about robust flavours. The food announces itself with the same trumpet fanfare you get in the corrida as the bull enters the arena. It is a wake-up call to appetite. The red and yellow colours of the national flag are often on the plate, too, with peppers and tomatoes and that utterly divine Iberico ham, the result of free-ranging, acorn-fed pigs.

We were both shy, spoke no Spanish, and so were hesitant in our approach. And this seemed to open something up in Spanish hearts, because we found a warm welcome. Jerez with its sherry bodegas and riding school appealed immediately. I recall a lunch where we were served slabs of tuna in a bean and tomato sauce topped with a fried egg served in an open earthenware bowl, and a glass of sherry to go with it. And a serving of *patatas bravas* on the side. Everything was just so, but in a wholesome home cooked way, with nothing of the French *haute cuisine* about it. Yet here was a dish to relish, mopped up with those potatoes and crusty bread moist within. It was a meal that demanded a siesta.

We looked in on the local bullfighting arena and then visited the great riding school of Jerez that rivals the Spanish Riding School in Vienna. And dare I say it, the *pre*-Andalusian horses were more to my taste, more elegant and not as blocky as the great white stallions of Vienna.

We enjoyed our time in Jerez and Cadiz, but it was in the small riverside town of Sanlúcar de Barrameda that we really hit the jackpot. We'd come to this unassuming place to see the riverside beach that is the site of an annual horse race, which sadly we missed, but as a consolation prize, there was a string of small fish restaurants that we got to know well, strung along the beach. These provided our plates with the result of the nearby fishing boats early morning trawl – the freshest fish and prawns imaginable, prepared over open fires and served with salads and chips. It was lovely weather, and the place cast such a spell on us that over the years we returned to it a number of times and introduced our children to it too. For them and us, it later became a place of memories for its sublime tapas, and molten chocolate dipped churros that they loved too.

Some years later, we had a beach holiday with our children near Javea on the Mediterranean coast, in which three images coalesce in my memory.

The first was a supermarket that had me salivating at the small mountains of prawns – three different sizes and varieties, alive and still moving. The price was a fraction of what we would have expected to pay in the UK, and I bought enough for a blow-out meal at our holiday cottage. After lunch we needed a walk, and made our way to the sea and found a pier on which a fiesta was taking place. We found seats in a stand of wooden bleachers and before us a scene took place which held us incredulous and not a little disturbed. It seemed almost mediaeval in intent, designed by Hieronymus Bosch, the Dutch painter of human folly. Groups of young men were running with bulls and cows along the pier. The idea was to make one of the animals give chase, and, before it could reach you, escape by diving into the sea. Quite often, the bull also ended up in the sea where it was herded by circling boats to a landing place at the end of the pier where the whole process was repeated. It must be said that no harm seemed to come to either humans or bulls, but we were dumbfounded. This was something from another age and mindset. How had this spectacle made it into the twentieth century at a beach resort on the Mediterranean? Travel, they say, broadens the mind and on that day our minds were indeed broadened in ways we had not expected. We had to accept that our norms were not the norms of everyone, certainly not the Spanish.

But back to that earlier trip *à deux* with Jan in the caravan in '85. We stopped in Cartagena and found ourselves embroiled in the great Catholic Festival of the Passion of Easter. It was creepy as hell. In the narrow winding streets of this city, amid a landscape of desolation, there was a great upwelling of popular feeling made evident on the streets at night as the Virgin of each church and cathedral was carried on huge weighty wooden platforms by struggling and sweating boys and men, seemingly almost crushed by the weight of it all. This highly organised and orchestrated religious hysteria travelled through the city in purple and white hooded robes, carrying burning torches ahead and behind the great cloth-swathed palanquins carrying the effigy of Christ's mother, spot-lit for effect. Drums beat a sombre rhythm as the palanquin with its religious cargo passed by in a slow, swaying motion. Every now and then from one of the overhanging wrought iron balconies a cry would ring out and the parade would halt, the palanquin placed on the ground as the singer on her balcony gave rein to her passion. It sounded like the tearing hell of a death in the family, and I suppose that is how it was for them. We were left uneasy and bewildered. We looked afresh the next day at the people in the streets, now returned to seeming normality. Who were these people so besieged by their emotions, going crazy at bullfights, at football games and in their streets before a wooden idol? It was as if the Middle Ages had not quite given up on Spain and the Catholic Church was still at its very core. We left with a feeling of puzzlement and relief and headed further up the coast into a more polyglot and touristed region.

We stopped at the lovely old Roman town of

Tarragona on the coast near Barcelona and ate a never-to-be-forgotten paella on a restaurant deck with a view of the Mediterranean. I love food that seduces you even before you've had one bite. And this paella in its copper pan, big enough to cross the English-French Channel, did just that. It had rabbit, chicken and prawns, onion and red peppers, but of course it was that rice infused with saffron, herbs and garlic that held it all together. It's not a complicated dish, but to get it right is not easy. This one had been slowly simmered over a wood fire, so it had a smoky quality which added depth and taste.

A few nights later, we were in the backstreets of Barcelona having drinks in a rather dodgy square when a number of tango dancers emerged and began their graceful performance, all formality and animosity, lust and rage, as we sipped beer and ate tapas. We felt that we were beginning to understand Spain, and it was an intoxicating feeling.

Our last meal in Spain on that caravan trip was a picnic beside the turquoise Lake of Banyoles, close to the Pyrenees and the old city of Girona. We had this gem-like place to ourselves in early May. All I can recall of the meal was good bread, cheese, fresh fruit, and a wonderful salami that shone ruby red when held up to the sun, which we relished. It was only some time later when Jan checked the label of the salami, that we discovered we'd feasted on donkey. Spain had had the last laugh, but considering the gifts it had bestowed on us over the years, we chose to laugh at ourselves.

Many years later, we piled into my old Mercedes CLS, the 'Black Banana' as I call it because of its curved shape, and drove down to see our daughter Imogen for a week at the Sant Roc Hotel in the small coastal town of Palafrugell. Here we finally had a meal that wiped the taste of donkey away forever.

This bewitching small white town has one of the prettiest seafronts imaginable, along a cliff-clad coast with small hidden inlets and Japanese landscapes filled with pines overhanging turquoise water. It is the Mediterranean that dreams are made of. On one cliff top walk, we passed two women photographing a young girl in a white bridal gown against this setting. At the end of the cliff-hung path, you reach a small gem of a sandy beach with stone stacks offshore, with one or more picturesque pines attached. After this walk, we returned to the small square above the town beach and had an outdoor lunch of sea bass and crayfish that overflowed our plates. It was perfection, and we sat on late into the afternoon, faces raised to the sun, sipping Sangria, all thoughts of donkey forgotten.

There may be a dark and savage side to the Spanish soul, but on an icy winter night in England when there is sleet on the wind and the threat of snow by morning, Spain's red and yellow nature calls to you with a siren song that is hard to ignore. We will be going back soon.

CHAPTER 18

THE ENGLISH PUB

After four decades in Britain, I still struggle to define the appeal of the pub, but am grateful that they form part of life here. There are doubtless doctoral theses on the role of the pub in Britain. I only speak as a foreigner who came to them at the age of 30 and liked what I found, a haven of civility generally, little if any demands made on you, no pretentions, and over the decades, increasingly good food. The local beer, flat English bitter, took much longer to appeal. It tasted like cat's piss, or what I imagined that would taste like. Funny how a taste creeps up on you. Today my favourite pub drink is a pint of Harvey's Bitter, with its lovely, floral, hoppy scent, brewed in Lewes just down the road. When I speak of pubs, my experience is almost exclusively that of the English country pub. These are no doubt very different to a Glasgow city pub on a Saturday night.

When we first got here – to Sussex that is – there were still many pubs that were the local boozer, where on entering you got an X-ray style once-over from the regulars and felt immediately that you had failed the test and were intruding. The hostility may have been muted, but it did not make you wish to return.

But, generally speaking, the pub is Britain's Happy Place.

The reasons for this are varied: the congenial atmosphere; the range of drinks on offer; often an attractive garden in the summer and roaring log fires in winter; wholesome, and in some cases outstandingly good, food. It's a non-judgmental kind of place, with no dress code. It's a neutral space for the community to meet, to socialise, to flirt, to fall in love and to get legless if they so desire – and this being Britain, legless is the aim of many. It's a clearing house for local news and gossip. In such a class-driven society as Britain remains, the pub is egalitarian and welcoming without any side, there are no questions about where you went to school, what you do for a living, or your accent or religion. It's just easy. And for the middle classes who still do dinner parties, with all the stress involved in that social adventure, the pub is a happy alternative where everyone pays their way and there is no pressure on the host, just the publican and his or her staff. I can't remember the last time we walked into a pub to see ten pairs of eyes sending hostile vibes our way. It is no longer the hideout for local yokels.

We have a few favourites locally, though it must be said that going to the pub for a meal is no longer a cheap outing. If a couple has a three-course meal with drinks and wine you can easily spend £100. Having a pint and a burger you could get away with £40. It is surprising what you can find in a country pub these days. The sophistication of the cooking has improved dramatically over the four decades we have lived in England. And after horse riding on the forest or a good long walk with the dog, a Sunday lunch at the Gallipot Inn, one of our regular watering holes, offers an intriguing and satisfying menu. At the end of the Pandemic year of lockdowns the pubs are opening again; we will be heading back to the Gallipot soon.

Here starters range from the Sussex smokie (smoked fish) or the delicious poached haddock with grain mustard, cream & cheddar gratin. Offal is not really my thing, but you may feel differently and enjoy the lambs' kidney – sautéed kidneys with Worcestershire sauce, red wine reduction & garlic toast. King scallops, seared with crispy ham, pesto & lemon dressing. There is also smoked duck with papaya and sweetcorn salsa And, finally, rabbit rissoles with aioli, orange

& rocket salad.

Main courses include a burger, fish and chips, lambs' liver and bacon. There is also seabass with lobster bisque on crushed new potatoes and fennel salad. There is a mixed seafood paella and of course the meat roasts which are the staple of weekend dining. These include lamb, beef and pork with all the trimmings.

And if after that you can still manage a pudding you will be spoiled for choice with the homemade selection. There is a delicious Baileys crème brûlée; a warm chocolate brownie with clotted cream, steamed ginger pudding with spiced rum sauce; a selection of sorbets or ice creams and my favourite: treacle tart with vanilla ice cream. After that a Sunday afternoon nap is not something you have to apologise for.

At the Gallipot, the Coach and Horses, great garden and food to match it, the Hatch Inn where you have to duck if you are over six feet tall, as this place has been in business since 1430, almost 600 years, and the Hurstwood, which offers a French bistro feel with a menu to match, we have celebrated birthdays, and Christmas and New Year meals out.

We are not regulars in the sense that the staff knows our names and we have our own tankards hanging behind the bar, but we get a nod and a smile at the ones we go to most frequently and that is a good feeling. There is something about sitting in the garden of the Coach & Horses at Chelwood Gate watching the sheep and lambs in the fields opposite, as you eat crisp succulent pork belly with a local cider, or maybe the fish barbecue at the slightly Yuppie-ish pub, the Griffin in Fletching with its sunset-facing garden or a wild winter's night at the Hatch Inn at Coleman's Hatch near Hartfield where you can imagine the ghosts of poets W.B. Yeats and Ezra Pound drinking cider by the fire as they did for three winters from 1913 to 1916, living nearby at Stone Cottage, and found it hard to go back to London after walking miles on the heath in the moonlight. Pound had his room upstairs and would hear Yeats reciting a new poem in his singsong Gaelic accent in the room beneath: two poets busy creating while just across the Channel men were dying in their millions.

Now and then in summer I will indulge myself if Jan is out at a Poetry Society meeting. I will make my way to the Anchor Inn at Hartfield, opposite the cricket ground, order a pint and the best burger available locally and then find a spot in the garden where the waitress will deliver the meal. Sitting there, a bit stiff from riding, basking in the late summer evening light, listening to the thwack of cricket balls striking willow, there is a deep quiet contentment to be had. This being southern England, nobody will bother you and you are left to enjoy the meal and your beer.

Around you there will be couples or family groups also enjoying being out and having a meal. Later, driving home with the windows down to catch the summer breeze, I feel at my ease, a small sense of holiday that occurs in a long marriage like ours, where we give each other space to be on our own now and then, riding out on a horse or visiting a friend or having a meal out at a pub. Cheers to this most civilised institution, the British pub.

Chapter 19

70th Birthday - 18 May 2020

(From: *Life in a Time of Plague* amid lockdown)

Finally, my birthday is here. I've made it to 70, despite the virus, and I am filled with gratitude, and something like a sense of achievement.

I have packed a fair bit into these seven decades, and I feel blessed. As I wake on this momentous day, I have so many mixed emotions. As ever, there is the feeling of awkwardness brought about by the knowledge that I will be the centre of attention today, and that always makes me nervous. So I am grateful for lockdown, as it eliminates any chance of parties or anything of that nature, which would just be embarrassing. And yet to be able to have had some sort of celebration, a meal out with family and friends, would have been good.

But the sun is up, and it is another beautiful day. Has there ever been a spring like it in England in the past forty years we've called it home? I don't think so; I certainly don't remember anything like this. The good weather has become so good that we now take it for granted, just like we did the Cape Town summers all those many years ago.

Jan brings me coffee, gives me a hug and wishes me

happy birthday. I am grateful to have her with me; we have walked a long and winding road together since I met her, aged 18, at the university where I had arrived as an older student. Her presence is the best gift of any I will receive this day. I know that even before I open my presents, which lie in a pile on the bed where she has placed them. We have lived together on three continents, Africa, Europe and North America, and we have created two amazing children who continue to astonish us. She has had much to contend with in our shared life. I have not been the easiest, kindest or most generous of partners. I come with a temper and many other failings, but throughout she has stood by me, even in our darkest times.

We lie in bed, sipping coffee, taking in the day and speaking a little of the past and about this strange day and its Covid-imposed stillness. There is a huge envelope among the presents, and I open it first and am amazed. It is a watercolour birthday card of me in all my ancient glory, sitting in my steamer chair with Callum looking over the stable door behind me at the top of the garden, Gus by my side and my trusty laptop on my knees, looking much as I have looked this past two and a half months while writing this book. Jan asked our friend, the artist Susie Rotberg, to produce this wonderful card, and she has done me proud. I now understand that their 'socially-distanced' walk yesterday with the dogs in the woods was also a handing-over of this spectacular card. The words inside are as beautiful and I am silenced, as ever, reading Jan's words.

And then the stillness is broken. The phone begins to ring, and the texts bearing good wishes pile in. It is like no other birthday I have known. Usually, I get calls from close family and a friend or two. This morning, the calls come non-stop from Cape Town, Santa Barbara, Bristol, with videos of siblings and family singing happy birthday, and texts and emails in the dozens.

One, from our daughter Imogen, in lockdown over near Rye with her godmother, brings me particular pleasure – wishing me a happy day and looking forward to another year. I wonder if she has any idea how much it means to me?

I eventually get into the shower and have breakfast

sitting in the sunshine in the living room. My presents, a bone china mug for my coffee, hand-painted with the blue agapanthus of my childhood, books and more books, lie all around me, nature and travel and food writing, my favourites. I have the joy of weeks of reading to look forward to. Later, I sit out in the garden and luxuriate in the warmth of the sun and the company of the busy, dancing, swooping swallows. Who needs a celebration when nature provides this display?

At 11am, Jan waves from the kitchen door, telling me to come down. I walk down the lawn and see my son Dominic and his partner Steph at the front door, loaded down with bags of food and drink and a huge cake box. I feel my throat constrict and my eyes prick with tears, which I hold back as hard as I can. With their help, Jan has orchestrated a truly splendid champagne picnic lunch which, sitting well apart, we enjoy under the Chinese dogwood tree. There is a huge salad to go with smoked salmon in dill, sourdough loaves, warm veggie quiches and fresh buttered asparagus. We eat and talk boats, and there is love and laughter, and I feel blessed, dear God, so blessed.

I am instructed to open another birthday card, this one from Dom, Jan and Steph, which this multi-talented woman has illustrated beautifully with travel scenes. It's my real birthday present. Inside, there are words that once more grab at my chest and constrict my throat. I read on through the blur. There is a choice of three gifts laid out within the card. I can choose between a sailing trip from Italy to Greece, a sailing trip up the Caledonian Canal in Scotland, or a trip along the Canal du Midi in a barge, an ambition of mine, long-held but given up on now, as I do not feel fit enough to cope with locks, steering and French challenges. These people know me so well, they are not surprised when I opt for the canal journey in France. Dom and Steph will do everything for us that is needed, managing the boat and the locks. I will be able to relax on deck like the Queen of the Nile. Who could resist?

And so my day passes in chapters of happiness that will be hard-wired into my memory for as long as it lasts. Today will be a memory I will cherish forever.

And then Jan disappears to get coffee. Minutes later, I'm told to shut my eyes, and I open them to find the biggest birthday cake I have ever seen before me, with 'Happy 70th Birthday Jules' piped on the top. It's from a French patisserie in Brighton, a huge cartwheel of a double sponge filled to bursting with raspberries and cream and topped with a fresh-glazed raspberry jam compote and seven candles. It is stunning. Enough for twenty-two servings they tell me as I start to cut huge slices that will reduce the servings by half. They laugh and we devour it and have seconds.

Happiness usually creeps up on you, or looking back, you realise you were happy at some point, unaware of it at the time. Today, sitting in the garden, happiness pours down on me like Victoria Falls in flood. We spend the afternoon lazily talking boats and boat journeys.

Dom and Steph leave in the late afternoon. Jan and I doze on the lawn, as this most perfect day draws to a close. And over more drinks Jan says she has one last surprise; she has conjured up a fresh duck from the high street butcher to roast for our dinner. I am so touched. It is my favourite, and is always our festive meal, but both of us are just too full from our long lunch, and we decide to freeze the bird for another time. There are only so many treats you can manage in one day.

I cannot help but contrast my day with the state of the world. We need to try harder, to be so much better. We have been given the gift of consciousness. What does that mean? It means that, unlike other animals, we know the score. We know we are going to die. We know we are failing. We know we are destroying our world. And so, as we know this, know it consciously, yet do nothing to help ourselves and our world, that is a death sentence written by ourselves. And it means we deserve to die as a species. It seems we have made a conscious decision to choose death, to choose annihilation. As a species, it seems we've opted for suicide. Is it self-hatred? It might very well be. It is a desperately sad thought. But I do not wish to end my day, this precious day, on such a miserable note.

As I collapse into bed, my mind wanders from the day just past to the past itself. This time in lockdown fosters daydreaming. But I've been doing that for seven decades now. It started by taking me out of my school desk in the Cape Town suburb of Newlands, out over the playing fields with their cricket pitches and up the mountain, to look out over the Cape Flats, the Hottentot Holland Mountains and the beaches on either side of the Peninsula, where I spent my time riding or fishing or swimming. This ability to wish myself away from the present became a lifelong habit; and this night, while tied down by Covid-19, it does not take much for my mind to get up out of bed to go walkabout, as the Aborigines like to say.

Inevitably, it takes me to my horse next door. In my mind's eye, it is once more early morning when I brush him down and saddle him up, and soon we are in the green tree tunnel down to the lake and up the hill past Susie and Ed's home, and then out into the open reaches of the forest itself, gorse, bracken, heather and grass, with the signature stands of dark brooding pines on the highest hills of the forest. These pine clumps look like meeting places for witches' covens or druidic ceremonies. Nothing grows beneath them because of the load of pine needles they shed, making the ground beneath infertile. It is dark and cool within the copses on a warm summer's day and cold, dark and windy in winter.

As this is daydreaming, time travel, my horse is on his best behaviour, moving smoothly through his paces as needed, shying at nothing, doing my bidding so as not to upset the flow of my thoughts, a moving meditation. We turn down into Five Hundred Acre Wood of Pooh Bear fame, and I note the lightning-struck beech tree that I think of as family. It is within its shattered trunk at human head height, six foot up, that Jan and I would hide one last special birthday or Christmas present for our children, gifts from Pooh Bear and his friends, Roo, Piglet and the donkey Eeyore. I smile, remembering their delight at sitting on my shoulders to find a gift once again. And I smile too, recalling the philosophical humour at the heart of A.A. Milne's books that kept parents reading, for the umpteenth time, to children also addicted to the stories.

Further on into the wood, there is a circle of giants, beech trees standing in what looks like a century-deep family conversation. And I know now that they are indeed talking;

science tells us so. Their root systems and the fungal fibres that bind them together underground are in effect a nervous system, a brain of sorts. A tree among them struck with an axe, or feeling fire, will telegraph the news to its neighbours. There is an intelligence at work.

As Callum and I step softly in among them, they pause their talk and listen. They know we are there, our footfall, almost a ton in weight, has been noted; it can scarcely be missed. And they are quite still, listening, waiting. They have no reason to trust man or horse; both have a history of damaging their kind, so they wait to see if these two, Callum and I, will do what we most do, stand and stare, before moving on to stroke a trunk, marking out the carved hearts and initials with a finger, nibble on bark or grab a mouthful of leaves. They sigh, but perhaps it is only the wind in their highest branches. Or maybe it is an exhalation of breath as they recognise me. After all, I have been coming here for decades. I have laughed here and cried here and prayed among them. They know me. I feel watched, in a benign way.

I pick up the reins, and the big copper horse strides ever deeper into the wood. I raise a hand to fend off a branch or to pluck a leaf. As we start to move downhill, I collect him, bringing his haunches in under him to make him careful of the ground. I do not want him to slip. We reach the pond, where we like to stop and watch the reflections, and then there is a good leg-stretching gallop up the hill, keeping an eye out for dog walkers all the while. This horse has a ground-eating length of stride like nothing I have ever known. Soon we have crested the hill and I let him blow to catch his breath; his flanks heave but soon settle; he is fit as a fiddle. He knows we are headed home; he has a compass in his head that set itself a month after arriving here, which tells him which direction home lies, wherever we are in the forest. And he knows every path, every fork and every turning, and will take it unswervingly if I give him his head. But he also likes to stop now and then, and just look.

His home-going stride lengthens into an almost running rhythm and I sit deep in the dressage saddle, feel the warmth of his flanks, the silken sway of his mane, the ears that seem to have a life of their own. It is not long before we are on the last hill home and then the stables come into view. I unsaddle, wash him down, mop his eyes and nose and put him back in his stable after checking his haynet and water.

I open my eyes, and look at the shadows on the ceiling above our bed; I have once more escaped lockdown for an hour, deep in the woods with Callum. It is a trick that never fails. My school taught me well.

I made it to 70! That is no mean achievement. There will be new challenges to face in the days that lie ahead, Covid-19 not least among them. But for now, I let slip the lines and feel the breeze take me out onto a dark sea. Who knows when or how the journey will end, but I will go with it.

Chapter 20

An American Breakfast, Lunch and Supper

My brother Herman and his wife Teri live in Santa Barbara, California, in a stunning house on a cliff overlooking the Pacific. So over the years we have got to know that part of America quite well. It is always a pleasure to return, knowing the local scene, where to go for walks, where the farmers' markets are held, where to shop and where to have breakfast out.

An American breakfast is always a pleasure. Maybe not something you want every day but once in a while, the mix of fresh orange juice, buttermilk pancakes, cream, maple syrup, eggs and bacon, or a huge omelette filled with onions, peppers and bacon is a pleasure. Now if you add sunshine and say the East Beach Café in Santa Barbara or the breakfast spot in the marina, The Breakwater, you have a start to the day that is pretty hard to improve on. The sea glints obligingly blue and the surrounding mountains are not yet covered in heat haze, but are a darker-hued mauve beneath the bluest blue sky. It's all sun gold and blue, and the tablecloth is that lovely pale buttery yellow that goes so well with white plates. Before you even sit down there is a sense of a real treat in store.

The very way the waitresses walk, a sort of business-like briskness, bringing menus and water or coffee, just adds to the pleasure, knowing you are in good hands. Once you've placed your order, all you have to do is to decide on the kind of bread for your toast, white, sourdough, brown, and about five other kinds. And then you can completely relax and sip your first coffee of the day.

Feeling free of the cares of home, some 6,000 miles away, only adds to the pleasure. And yet, because we have had family here this last few decades, this place is a kind of second home. The masts of the nearby yachts wave slowly in the breeze and bob gently, adding a salty maritime note to the setting.

The breakfast arrives on warm plates that almost overflow with good things and a long slow pleasure begins. It is so good! And then more coffee and a much-needed stroll along the beach to find a spot to chill and read. There is movement in and out of the harbour to observe, fishing boats and yachts, and there is also much evidence of wildlife. Huge sea lions loll on the buoys and above the beach, flights of pelicans flap by, looking like seaplanes landing in flotillas. It is all too easy to shut your eyes and doze off.

Maybe it is the sea air and the sense of holiday that adds edge to appetite and by lunchtime you are hungry again. Luckily the pier is close to hand and amid the surfboards on the walls and the monkey-nut shells beneath your feet, you find the laid-back vibe of the Longboard Restaurant. The choice ranges from locally caught fish, calamari, shrimp and lobster, alongside the usual burgers and steaks. After that breakfast, a piece of fresh grilled fish, coleslaw and a shared portion of chips is more than enough.

To work off the calories, we hire one of those tourist bikes which you pedal side by side and explore the waterfront and downtown area with its royal palm trees and buskers.

Night on this coast can be cool and after a sunset drink at the Boat House it's back to the marina for a warming candlelit dinner at Brophy's, with its stunning views out across the harbour at dusk. Here awaits an American version of *bouillabaisse* – and no worse for that – *cioppino* is of Italian origin, out of San Francisco, and offers a huge bowl full of mussels, crab, fish, clams, calamari, tomato and wine topped with Parmesan. It is rich in all that this sea can provide, and soon enough you feel pretty damn Pacific yourself.

Early the next morning, you join the whippet-thin women walking their dogs on the beach as the early-morning pelican squadrons sail overhead, catching the breeze lifting off the sea cliffs. And then, forgive me, but it's back to the marina for one last American breakfast.

Living as he does two miles from the harbour in Santa Barbara, Herman has the sea treasure chest of the Pacific upended at his feet anytime he chooses to walk to the dockside. Saturdays, for him, invariably include the purchase of some of the freshest fish, salmon, seabass, rock fish or tuna and a spider crab whose carapace is the size of a handbag and legs that stretch out to cover the dimensions of the wheel of a horse carriage, and for good measure, a bunch of the hugest oysters I've ever seen, the size of revolvers. This wild feast is well suited to Herman's character, as like mine it includes something of the savage, as anyone who has ever questioned his heritage has found out in short order. He steams the crab in a sort of cannibal pot, and the smell envelopes the house and the neighbourhood. The fish and, surprisingly, the oysters, go on the barbecue. This array is then served for lunch on Saturday with salads, fresh bread and a few pints of drawn garlic or plain butter sauce. Then it's time to roll up your sleeves and make a pig of yourself, making damn sure to stay apace of Herman and his family. When you finally look up and draw breath it's to see an array of butter glistening lips all around you, like a pride of African lions, licking the blood of a buffalo off their chops. And there is the same food-dazed look on all faces, mine most of all.

As I've got older, I increasingly hear my mother's voice in my head. She too loved her food but also loved fashion. Her passions were at odds with each other and she ate carefully. Now and then she would say to me, '*Es es mein kind!*' in the Yiddish words of my father's family, urging me on to eat. And speaking for herself, she would say after a particularly delicious meal, 'I could eat that all again!'

I would have loved to show her this coast all the way up Big Sur and beyond, to the place that stole my heart,

Mendocino, beloved of artists and writers, a place where big surf booms and surges against the sea cliffs and a white clapboard town huddles above, offering a certain boho charm.

And speaking of family, I can't leave Santa Barbara without mentioning a charming and very enterprising place owned and run by one of Herman and Teri's daughters, Lindsay, and her husband Seth.

They fell in love with home brewing while busy with high-flying careers in New York in finance and fashion, but gave that up to open their own pub, micro-brewery and restaurant in downtown Santa Barbara. The Brass Bear Brewing and Bistro is quite something if you miss a pint of real beer. Their own IPA, The Hopping Grizzly, will put hair on any man's chest and there are nine more beers to pick from. This rustic spot is no tourist trap, but a locals-only favourite and if it's a relaxing evening out you are looking for this place is well worth a visit.

Wine drinkers are also well catered for with a range of local wines and some from further afield. Here you will find a menu of all locally sourced products from skewers of beef, chicken or veg, alongside Seth's Virginian potato cakes, and a salad.

Herman keeps going back for skewers of peri-peri prawns that reignite his South African taste buds with distant memories of the same dish served by the Portuguese in Lorenzo Marques, now Maputo.

Teri likes the Blond Ale and the slim rods of spicy roasted zucchini. Good old toasted cheese sandwiches with rich Cheddar cheese and Prosciutto is a great bite to have with a beer and you will be in luck if they are serving their smoked ribs. Alabama, look out – this stuff is the real finger licking deal.

You eat well on this coast that informed the food revolution that changed American cuisine. It's all here, locally grown, caught and produced. The quality of the raw ingredients offered to chefs rivals what is available in France.

But if there is one piece of fish that calls loudest to me when I am once more under the California sun, it is a fishy immigrant from South Africa, a musselcracker that is mounted in my brother's living room, as though to mock me on every visit. For if the truth be told, that musselcracker is rightly mine. Herman hooked it yes, but I risked my life and limb to pluck it from the sucking waves that threatened to wash both the fish and me back into the sea after the hook came out and the huge flapping toothy beast was slip-sliding its way back into the briny. With water churning around my legs, I made damn sure that fish stayed caught, so mine by right and by every tenet of justice. And yet it hangs to this day in Herman's home.

In the 65 years of Herman's life, he and I have never had an argument, not once. And so it shall remain. But every now and then I like to remind him that the musselcracker is only on loan to him, until such time as he sees the error of his ways, and justice prevails, his wrong-headedness ends, honour is finally observed, and that fish crosses the Atlantic to my home in Sussex. As yet, he has not given up on his claim. Fishermen are like that – dogged. So to assuage my pain, I allow him to pay for most of my meals while I am in Santa Barbara and those breakfasts, lunches and suppers taste all the sweeter for it. In fact, I have decided to let him keep my fish, as I have dined out a hundred times more than that fish is worth. I've got the better part of the deal, and he is lumbered with that guilt-inducing musselcracker.

If ever you find yourself in Santa Barbara, make your way to his home on Shoreline Drive and ask to see this famous fish. You will get a very old-fashioned welcome from Herman, but he will nevertheless take the time to show you 'his' fish and to justify his ownership and to blacken my name, but now you know the truth. If pushed, he may even take you out to lunch. If so, do order the lobster at Brophy's. I can recommend it.

CHAPTER 21

FIRST CATCH YOUR CALAMARI - ANGOLA 1967

From: *A Fisherman in the Saddle*
For my sister Janine

There are moments in life that pass us by and it is only years later, on reflection, that the true value, significance or importance of that day's events are finally appreciated. And then there are events which impact us for life and which we are conscious of at the time, as being life-changing in some way. This story is about one of the latter such events in my life. When I look back, I see it in full colour and as if in a Roman frieze, the dark outline of men carrying poles seen against an almost impossibly blue sea.

This particular day's events impacted my culinary taste and sensibility, my appreciation of beauty, my understanding that there were societies that lived differently to my own, and that they were profoundly worth understanding. This day was one in which time stopped briefly and added to my slim weight of knowledge and built a desire to know more about the world outside of my own. You may say that my mind became more inquiring, and this may have directed me in time to a life in journalism with a particular interest in anthropology, the seas and not least, food. It is a substantial load for any one day to carry and yet it is no less than true.

The city of Luanda, the capital of Angola in 1967, glittered in the heat, a hard white against rampant green vegetation with a deep blue bay beyond, graced by a palm-fringed island barrier reef. It seemed as if most human life here came on two wheels; there were motorbikes everywhere, like schools of fish round pavement café peninsulas. Parked in their thousands, they formed an effective crash barrier between strolling pedestrians, motorists and more motorcyclists.

I was 17 years old and away from home for the first time with an American classmate of mine who was dating my 15-year-old sister. I had been invited to spend three weeks with him and his family in Angola, where his father ran the Kabinda oil fields for Texaco. I was not that sure about it, playing gooseberry to him and my sister, but I had been promised some great fishing and that clinched it for me. And besides, my parents would not allow my sister to go on her own.

The heat struck you like a wall as you stepped from the small, air-conditioned Fokker Friendship aircraft out into the West African sunshine. It was seriously hot. A thick, wet, cloying heat that made the air seem tangible. You felt as though you were pushing through some foreign substance that yielded, just, to force. On the airport concourse there was evidence of another force; Portuguese troops in olive green fatigues were everywhere, carrying Uzi submachine guns. On the way through the city approaches, we saw bullet-riddled traffic signs, where these young Portuguese conscripts had been doing a bit of target practice.

I was still trying to regain my equilibrium, lost as the aircraft dived over the statue of Christ on the hills above Suda Madeira a few hours before and a couple of hundred miles to the south, refuelling and picking up some new passengers.

The pace of life in Luanda was slow; not surprisingly in this humid heat, pedestrians strolled at a languid pace. The place had something of Lisbon and Nice about it, a shared cosmopolitanism, though it would be many years before I could make that judgement myself. The shops were chic, and the pedestrians predominantly short, dark Portuguese men in cream tropical-weight suits. Their hair, moustaches and shoes all shone immaculately. There were few Portuguese women about. The black residents of Luanda looked decidedly less cowed than those in my country, though soldiers lounged on street corners, guns slung casually from shoulders, looking bored. The boredom would not last; 500 years of simmering anger at colonialism was on a rolling boil. The masters were about to be mastered, looking back briefly at paradise lost, and then going, but not before doing their best to destroy all that they left behind. Every piece of machinery or engineering kiboshed in some way.

But for now, the war was 300 miles inland, and Luanda was at peace, or seemingly so. Carlo Ponti and Sofia Loren had just built a house next door to the Club Nuval (the naval club) on the waterfront. The place was exotic yet off the map, a great hideaway for those in the know.

The car bringing us from the airport pulled up at a white house that was almost overtaken by its garden, lush rubber plants, tall palms and bougainvillea almost enveloped it. We unpacked, showered and then headed down to the harbour to inspect the family's speedboat at the naval club. It was an unostentatious but perfectly serviceable speedboat which in the days to come would carry us backwards and forwards to Mussulo, the 25-mile-long sandy peninsula which followed the coastline about three miles offshore. This palm-bedecked strip of land was a pristine, white sandy paradise. Some of the palms leaned out almost horizontally over the beaches that faced back towards the mainland coast. You could sit in these trees, shaded by the fronds, and dangle your feet in the water, where they would be inspected by small fry. It was the kind of setting beloved by fashion photographers, but it was as far from fashion as it was possible to be.

The place was not more than 10 feet above the lagoon it had created on its landward side and the Atlantic, 100 yards beyond. It was home to a fishing tribe that scratched a living here, with a few chickens adding some meat to their diet. There was the odd pie dog and many small children.

We would start each day by taking the boat over to one or other of the fishing villages on Mussulo to arrange lunch. The menu was unchanging, barbecued chicken or fish or squid. Then we'd spend the morning fishing, swimming and water-skiing. It made for an idyllic holiday. If you had had enough of the boat, you could be dropped at one of a hundred beaches with a book, a cooler bag of Cokes and beer and, in places, blue mangrove crabs for company.

It was all low-key and very relaxed. In town, we were shown around the astonishing botanical garden where thirteen shades of bougainvillea, from purest white through cream, to salmon, to peach, apricot, and pink, finally reaching a deep burgundy. We walked round the fifteenth-century fort built by the Portuguese to command the harbour and roadstead, and visited the Catholic cemetery where many of the dead had better above-ground accommodation than the city's slum dwellers. The cinemas came as a revelation; marble, mahogany and ivory, with deep, velvet, plush seats, but without a roof, just the magnificence of the southern night sky. The short rainy season made this possible, a simple, temporary roof being needed to last no more than a couple of weeks.

But as usual, it was the action in the water that really gripped my attention. The sea world below that blue mirror of the bay hid myriad treasures, two of which would remain with me for life.

One morning, as usual, we took the boat over to Mussulo and at our favourite village asked if they could arrange lunch for us that day – squid for a change. A few hours later, we tied up again beneath the overhanging palm trees and saw a line of men, each with a ten-foot pole, marching one behind the other into the water. They walked out until they had created a wall of men in the shape of a 'u', starting with one man just ankle deep off the beach at each end of the curve, the rest progressively deeper with the deepest showing just their heads above water.

This human 'u' then began drumming their poles on the seafloor and walking slowly in towards the beach. As those who had been furthest out reached waist height, the colour of the sea within the 'u' began to darken. I wondered what this could possibly be. I did not have long to wait. As the back wall of the 'u' reached the beach, a few dozen squid shot out of the water and up the beach, still pumping their black ink behind them. They were dispatched, cleaned, and grilled on the spot over charcoal. It remains the freshest calamari I have ever eaten; seasoned simply with salt and pepper, the fire-blackened white tubes were succulent and meaty. They came with fire-baked bread and a salad of tomatoes of various colours, from yellow to red to green.

The sense of finally being in the real Africa, not the south of France in Africa that the Cape seemed to be, but something harsher, more complex, more tribal and ancient. As I lay on my towel digesting this extraordinary meal, chased out of the ocean just minutes before, I felt a strange sense of privilege that my life could offer me such an experience and that for all my whiteness and youthful gaucheness I was also a part of this continent, however semi-detached that might be.

That afternoon, I hooked and landed a bonito, a fish I'd not heard of before. Firm fleshed and tuna-like, it was served that night with fresh limes from the family's garden.

On our last day in Luanda, we experienced something extraordinary, provided by the natural world. Once more, we were out on the boat, this time past Mussulo, in the ocean proper. It was evening and a low sun shone a gentle light into the sea. Someone shouted, 'Look!' and as we glanced down into the water, we saw massive black shapes gliding beneath us They were manta rays, black on top and white underneath, swimming in a vast school of hundreds. They were so close to the surface that the water seemed to form a fine skin over their bodies, and as their wings lifted on the upward beat, all around us were hundreds of white wingtips raised as though in greeting.

After that initial shout, there was total and complete silence on the boat, despite its load of teenagers. We stared in awe. When the last of the rays had gone, still quiet, we turned and headed back for the harbour, and shortly after, flew home to the Cape and school in South Africa.

Those three weeks in Angola had introduced me to fish, fruits and vegetables new to me, and to a culture so different to my own and in some subtle way that I did not understand, I was changed by this experience more than I realised. My world view had changed, matured, the colours of my consciousness had also darkened slightly, as the waters of the lagoon had changed colour with the black ink of the incoming squid.

As the Portuguese fought and lost their colonies in Africa, both Mozambique and Angola, I realised that however much of a lotus land it had appeared to me, it was not something whose stability could be relied on, it was not a permanent state of being. And this made me realise that my own society was just as much subject to the same pressures, and it too was vulnerable. My political outlook was changed. That day on the beach at Mussulo was steeped in yellow sun, like a bee caught in amber, but the lesson it taught me was that I must prepare for change, that my privilege was a gift lent to me, not something I could rely on, and that my future in Africa was not assured.

CHAPTER 22

DRIVE-IN DELIGHTS

There is something about drive-in restaurants which appeals to me greatly. McDonalds, who are masters of human psychology, understand this very well and have made a killing with their version of the concept.

The pleasure lies in the privacy involved. Not having to get out of your car, deal with people and waiters and all the social interaction of eating in public. You stay in your bubble and enjoy your solitary pleasure. I suppose it is not the full Monty, not the three-course sit down deal, but a shortcut to a very private pleasure.

My introduction to this vice was by my mother who would take us kids to the Doll House in Mouille Point by the Lighthouse, a suburb of Cape Town, for a bite after an afternoon movie. We would get there between 5.30pm and 6pm and order hot dogs and milk shakes all round.

We thought both food and drink outstanding, and the occasion was always seen as a glorious treat. No wonder I was hooked young on drive-ins. It all seemed quite glamorous. The waiter in his whites coming to your car to take your order. And when he brought it out to you on a silver tray that clipped to a side window, the excitement in the car was palpable. Each hot dog came wrapped in a thick white napkin, and the milkshakes, vanilla, chocolate, or strawberry, were thick enough to allow a straw to stand erect for the duration of the drink. It was childhood heaven.

There were six lanes for parking, and as those ahead of you left, you moved your own vehicle forward. It was as slick as clockwork. As the meal was demolished, there would be one additional pleasure if the weather was misty or foggy. The adjacent red and white candy-striped foghorn would let out its moaning warning, along with a flash of light every few seconds, to all ships in Table Bay. Hot dogs without a foghorn somehow don't seem the same to this day. Once in a while, my mother would share a banana split with us, and then our cup truly overflowed.

As we drove away from the Doll House, all three of us in my mother's cramped Karmann Ghia, deliciously full and content, would nod off and by the time we got home to Newlands on the other side of the Table Mountain more than one of us would be fast asleep.

We lost touch with this wonderful drive-in as we grew up, and I think it finally closed when I was in my late teens. But help was at hand in Constantia, where another drive-in restaurant of a much more sophisticated kind had opened.

Now and then, after a night out with friends or on a date that included a few hours' dancing in a disco or nightclub, I would find myself headed home to my cottage, and suddenly crave something to eat. It was also a means of extending the evening, and the drive-in was the answer. There were seldom more than one or two other cars there around midnight when I would pull in and ask for my regular order – grilled lamb skewers, (or their excellent burger) French fries and an Appletiser. The food would arrive on a disposable tray, and I then had the pleasure of this solitary midnight feast in the quiet heart of a summer's night.

It gave me a chance to play the night over in my mind while enjoying the food. There was something terribly sophisticated, I felt, about this end-of-the-evening ritual. If I had been out on a date, my thoughts would dwell on the girl I had been with. I smoked in those halcyon days when we were all powered by the Sixties, and we were going to live forever and change the world. After the meal, I would light a cigarette and have five more minutes before heading up the hill and home to bed. In those last few minutes, some sense of peace would arrive and I would glimpse a bigger picture, confused as life still was for me, a jumbled kaleidoscope of images, thoughts and feelings. But with the newly arrived calm would come a sense, out of the dark and the sheer magnificence of the southern night sky in those pre-light pollution times, that all was well, and that I should simply continue to continue and things would become clearer in time.

I suppose these interludes in my late teens and early twenties gave me an appreciation of eating alone in my car, the radio pumping out late night music, and a chance, a space to think my thoughts and savour the night, the evening past, my youth, and the possibilities that life held. It was a deeply happy thing to do, and its effect was always slightly intoxicating in a strange way. The drive home with the windows open, letting in the summer scents of the gardens and vegetation, would wrap up another good evening and I would hit my bed content.

I would be lying if I did not admit that there were nights out and dates during which I longed for the moment when I would be free once more to pull into the Constantia drive-in for a date with a lamb kebab with which I had so much more in common than with my companion that night. And the satisfactions it offered so much more pleasurable and with no strings attached.

The drive-in restaurant is a much maligned and little understood institution. They are forever a cherished part of my youth and childhood. And when I look back at who I was back then, I often see myself in that drive-in, more at peace with myself than during the working day, and happy to be alone in the night.

Chapter 23

Secret Pleasures

What is your secret food delight? The things you'd be a bit ashamed to admit to, or at least to admit to when asked by anyone who is serious about food? Everyone has a few. In fact, there are countries that are almost defined by their secret and not so secret delights. Take Scotland for instance, with its battered, deep-fried Mars Bars and marginally more acceptable haggis, made of minced sheep's guts and rolled oats, and hand-moulded into a ball of deliciousness, if you are so minded. It's amazing what some people will put in their mouths.

One of my own secret delights has been off the menu for over a year now because of the pandemic. I've got a thing for the baked-on-the-premises steak pies offered by the Marks & Spencer food outlets at petrol stations. As my two or three visits to petrol stations this past year have been a flying pit stops, using a debit card to pay at the pumps, I have missed those pies. They are fresh baked, not reheated, and so they take me right back to my childhood visits to my father's bakery. These pies are a slim flattened oblong, rather than the deep oval pies of my early years, but they are pretty good all the same. And to this list of secret enjoyments, let's add sausage rolls and pork pies. I thank God for Greggs when hitting the UK motorways. A prawn sandwich is pretty good too, but baked meat goods are a particular weakness. I'm not proud.

Staying with meat-based secret pleasures is one I share with every South African, almost without exception. This is biltong, dried beef or game, and also its cousin, dried sausage. Both are fantastic snacks to eat on the go, or as good to have with drinks, but they are always welcome. The problem is keeping them in the house long enough, as the stuff is snaffled almost as soon as it arrives. This is South African soul food, and it harks back to the hunting, shooting days of previous centuries. It was also a staple of the Boer cavalry in their fight against the British colonisers who went to war in their wish to control the gold and diamond discoveries in the two Boer Republics. Those dried meat rations kept the Boer fight on the road for years and when I snack on a stick of biltong it is they who come to mind. It is filling and satisfying and both dried beef and dried sausage have a mouth feel that makes for good eating, a fantastically intense flavour.

And who would say no to hot fish and chips, liberally sprinkled with salt and vinegar? This is one of my favourite road meals, filling, delicious and economical. How many hot cooked meals can you buy for under £5? It always has the feel of being a special treat and yet it's available on every high street and side street in Britain and on the menu of pubs and restaurants.

And then of course, inevitably, there are the sweet things. This for me is led by chocolate, Mars Bars, slabs of Cadbury's Fruit and Nut, and Cadbury's Flakes. I'm not a fan of dark chocolate in any form, not with salt, or chilli or mint added. And ideally the chocolate should be just out of the deep freeze, crisp, hard and cold. Let's add fudge, nut brittle and rum and raisin ice cream to this list, while we are about it.

Just before lockdown, I noticed that I had been rumbled by the management of Morrison's Supermarket in Crowborough – they knew all about one of my vices. Proof was there right before my eyes, just by the entrance and before the fruit section. Knowing I would pass this way, they had cunningly put out a display of fantastic toffee apples, those red-glazed candy apples which shatter as you bite into them, the shards of caramelised red sugar mixing with the tart apple. Utterly delicious. It must be said that all of these things taste better when eaten alone. After all, they are a complete indulgence and so best kept secret.

The word indulgence is the key to all this. And in this context is the very opposite of the Catholic version. One particularly well-known Catholic method of exploitation in the Middle Ages was the practice of selling indulgences, a monetary payment or penalty, which supposedly absolved you of past sins and/or released you from purgatory after death.

But my form of indulgence does give a nod to a pleasure beyond simple appetite. When eating these secret pleasures, you enter a mental space, free for a moment of all concern. These particular favourite foods trigger things in my brain which bring with them a feeling of content and of peace, a moment stolen from the stress of life. So maybe there is method in my madness, a release from purgatory for a while, as toffee apples, steak pies and Flakes take effect?

I'm not in favour of food rules; a little of what you fancy does you no harm. And if I have to diet, which on occasion I have had to, then bread goes out the window, my carb of choice as the son of a baker, even though toast with butter heads my list of secret, and not so secret pleasures.

It is a never-ending source of amazement that you seldom see someone really overweight in France, despite all those croissants, baguettes, pains au chocolat and pains au raisin, despite every main dish with a sauce and wine, glorious wine, with breakfast, lunch and supper. How do they do it? And if the French have a secret national indulgence, what is it? I would dearly love to know.

It seems that I inherited my appetite for secret food pleasures. Once, when looking for my father's Swiss army knife in his bedside cabinet, to my amazement I found the drawers stuffed with chocolate bars, meebos (dried fruit rolls) and some biltong. This must have been his midnight feast stash and good luck to him, he made it to the ripe old age of 91 despite having Type 2 diabetes and died one night after entertaining his late-life lady love (known to the family as Utti van Tutti) to a slap-up Sunday lunch of grilled crayfish. We heard shortly after his funeral that she was targeting fresh meat in the Jewish old age home.

Years previously, my dad and his fishing pal, Pascoe Grenfell, arranged an oyster feast for themselves at Hamerkop on the Bredasdorp coast where my father had a fishing shack. There was a by-law in the deeds of the place that nobody would remove the teeming oysters off the rocks without the permission of the senior partner in this fishing venture, a huge bear of a man, Ferdie Bergh, a former Springbok Rugby player. But one day my dad and Pascoe decided to indulge themselves in this plentiful crop of bivalves, as Ferdie was not around. They had a ghillie bring them a few dozen each and pigged out.

The next day, feeling rather fragile and a touch liverish, they were horrified when Ferdie arrived unexpectedly and in a spirit of generosity promised them an oyster feast that night. My father begged off, pleading a stomach upset, and poor Pascoe had to man up to a table groaning with oysters, bread and butter, lemons and Tabasco sauce. Tucked into my bed and watching from the corner of the fishing cabin, my respect, love and affection for Pascoe rose another notch as he matched Ferdie, oyster for oyster. Secret indulgences do sometimes come at a price.

Chapter 24

A Warming Winter Breakfast

I used to hate porridge. There is nothing worse than the tasteless sludge served half cold, congealed, with a skin on it and a dollop of cold milk on top of it. I don't know when I returned to porridge or why. It was certainly some years ago and I was probably out of bread for toast, my usual go-to breakfast of choice, with butter, marmalade and coffee.

My dislike of porridge had been further compounded by what South African army cooks did to this health-giving grain. They produced it in huge metal 'pig pans' and by the time we were invited to serve ourselves it had taken on a blue-grey look that did nothing for the appetite or the taste, if you were bold enough to break the skin.

On that breadless morning, on which I probably did not have bacon and eggs either, my thoughts might well have turned to Pascoe Grenfell, my dad's old fishing partner and my childhood hero for so many reasons, all of them good. He had been the Wing Commander of a Spitfire Squadron and was kind, patient and encouraged me in all aspects of fishing. At the end of his life, I heard that he was fond of porridge and would eat it sometimes more than once a day.

So the combination of nothing in the larder and this warming childhood memory of Pascoe led me to search for porridge oats among the cupboards and shelves of our kitchen. And sure enough, there was a barely used box of porridge oats on a top shelf. The image on the box was of a laughing man of a previous century in antique clothing that included some tartan.

I'm not a great one for recipe reading, as you can probably tell if you've followed me thus far, but in this instance, I did read the words on the box and they were enlightening in offering suggestions as to what I might add to the grey sludge. In seven minutes, having mixed the oats with boiling water I had a good slow popping boil going on and I was stirring gently. I added a good pinch of salt to the pot, a knob of butter, a tablespoon of honey, and kept stirring.

After a minute more, I switched the heat off the hob and went to peer into the fridge to see if there was anything else I might tip into the porridge. I found half a punnet of large blueberries and I tipped them in too, stirring them into the mix. And then I added a dram of Scotch and stirred some more. I had a warm deep bowl waiting into which I decanted the porridge and for good measure added a dollop of clotted cream drizzled with honey.

It won't surprise you if you are already a porridge eater, but I polished that bowl off in record time. And I loved it. The combination of grains and fruit, dairy, salt and honey with the kick of Scotch, made for something utterly delicious and completely different to any porridge I had previously tried. I imagined Pascoe giving me a conspiratorial wink as I ate.

Nowadays, when I pull back the curtains and I see frost on the lawn, or snow, or even just miserable rain, my thoughts turn instantly to porridge. Before going off to feed my horse I will steep a few handfuls of porridge in boiling water, so that when I get back the work of making this morning manna is already half done.

And this stuff is seriously good for you – maybe more so if you hold back on some of the butter and cream – but don't do that on my behalf please. I think it's all good stuff.

I so enjoyed my experience of 'porridge-plus', shall we call it, that I did some research – OK, I Googled it – and once again I found myself surprised. The stuff is a super food.

There are no fewer than nine health benefits to eating oats and oatmeal. First of all they are incredibly nutritious. They are rich in antioxidants. They contain a powerful soluble fibre called beta-glucan. The stuff lowers your cholesterol levels. It's good for improving blood sugar and the clincher for me is that besides being very filling and satisfying, it can even help you to lose weight. I mean, what is not to like?

I wondered about Pascoe's passion for porridge and so asked the question – what happens if we eat oats three times a day? The benefits, it would appear, of eating oatmeal more than once a day include lowering your risk of heart disease and colorectal cancer. Whole grains, like oats, can also help reduce blood pressure and aid in digestion. Oatmeal can definitely be part of a healthy diet.

How is it, I wondered, that I had, to hit my sixties before discovering this wonder-food in my kitchen cabinets? In a world hooked on non-gluten foods here was another benefit. Oats are among the healthiest grains on earth. They're a whole grain and a great source of important vitamins, minerals, fibre and antioxidants.

I was so blown away by the magic of oats that I started looking out for recipes that included oats and I found a recipe for using oats to crumb fried chicken. Simply dip the chicken into milk or lay it in buttermilk for an hour and then roll it in oatmeal and shallow or deep fry. The result is sensational crumbed chicken that is healthier than normal. So, now I had breakfast and lunch sorted, how about supper, I wondered? I didn't have to look hard – battered fish with oatmeal and sauce tartare is scrumptious, in fact one of the best ways to eat fish in my opinion.

It is more than surprising that it has taken me so long to understand and appreciate the value of oats, for after all, if I have had one great passion in this life it has been horses. I have ridden horses since the age of six, when my father bought me a pony called Duke. In the subsequent sixty-five years I have had ample time and opportunity to observe the effect of oats on horses. In short, it drives them crazy with energy, has them literally jumping out of their skins. It is the stuff that powers racehorses and most working horses get some kind of oats in their feed. But you have to be careful, because this is dynamite food. Give them too much and they become almost unrideable, they will buck, rear, and bolt off with you if overfed on oats. Each horse has its own threshold that must be worked out.

I own a big 18-hand Irish Sports horse who is half warmblood and the oats will ignite that warmblood into boiling hot blood. I can only give him a scoop of hard food containing oats once a day, otherwise he gets the wrong idea about who is the boss in our partnership, ideas totally beyond his station. So really, I should have sussed oats out years ago, but it never crossed my mind. That has changed belatedly.

These days, the box of oatmeal has demands made on it that I could never have imagined in decades past. My health would have been improved, no doubt, if this discovery had not had to wait until I was in my seventh decade.

Pascoe Grenfell, bless his memory, he knew a thing or two, I can tell you.

Chapter 25

A Vegetarian Revolution

I so regret the vegetarian revolution, even as I acknowledge that it is morally, spiritually and healthwise an unalloyed good. And it will contribute significantly to saving the planet, as the production of meat and milk is a huge methane gas producer and forest destroyer.

We are living on the cusp of a change as profound in its way as that faced by our human forbears, the hunter gatherers, who came across the agrarian revolution some 12,000 years ago – farmers staking a claim to the territories of the hunters to grow grains and raise sheep and goats. It did not go down well with the hunters and doubtless took centuries to work out. We are now living through a gentler version of this huge gustatory change, which can only benefit our own health and that of the planet and leave us morally and spiritually better off. I am all for it but not without some longing and some lingering backward looks to a time of a chicken in everyone's pot and a roast leg of lamb or a beef joint on Sunday.

I feel much as St Augustine felt when he said: 'Make me chaste Lord, but not yet.' I am of a generation of meat eaters who, like Moses, have seen the Promised Land, but will not get to enter it. Our habits hold us hostage. So I will be eating steak and meat stews to the end of my time, probably shortening my life considerably. But when you get to the age of seventy and your knees are killing you, arthritis is curling your hands into claws, and your heart and blood are misbehaving, the flashing exit signs are a welcome distraction.

The truly woke and politically correct among us would do well to skip this paragraph as they will not be amused by it. I, however, found it very funny, as it reminded me so powerfully of the food culture in which I grew up in South Africa. Sholto, a colleague of mine at Bonhams, the international auction house where we both worked for many years, once told me a story about the annual camping holiday of a group of South Africans in Suffolk. It was a men-only affair, friends and relations of the woman he was going to marry, and his invitation was in a way an opportunity for them to give him the once-over.

It was a most convivial affair, he said, with all the tents drawn up into a great circle, in the middle of which was the barbecue or braai pit as it's known in the old country. There was a tall wooden stake in the middle of the circle on which a large tomato was impaled. After some days of a diet of grilled red meat with potatoes, bread or rice Sholto was desperate for a bit of green and asked the chef of the day if there was any salad to be had? The chef said no, but added that he could let him have the next best thing, a piece of chicken. Suddenly Sholto understood the significance of that impaled tomato. It was a long week, he said. But good lad that he was, he married the woman anyway. Luckily, she is a doctor, so hopefully she will regulate his diet in a more enlightened way.

But now the vegetarian front line has moved much closer to me personally. Our son Dominic has fallen in love with the loveliest woman imaginable, Stephanie, who has utterly stolen our hearts too. There is just one catch: she is a vegetarian. This presents problems, not insuperable ones, but problems, nevertheless.

I find that to produce a palatable vegetarian dish requires considerably more thought and attention than your average meat and two veg meal. It is no good cooking as normal and serving your son's girlfriend with the potatoes and broccoli that accompany your own meat dish. So I have become better acquainted with courgettes, aubergine and pulses.

There are certain simple vegetarian things that I truly love. The first is a proper Greek salad eaten in Greece. It does not taste the same anywhere else. It's got something to do with eating it on holiday in that embracing warmth and peace; something to do with the sprinkle of herbs on the slab of white salty sheep's cheese, the quality of the olive oil and the flavour of the tomatoes, the counter-note of the pale green pepper, the tart red onion. Eaten with a hunk of fresh Greek bread, this is pure pleasure. And alongside a plate of crumbed deep-fried baby calamari (if that is allowed) even better. And for dessert, another Greek concoction, that thick yogurt of theirs with fresh fruit, honey and nuts. And if you are really pigging out, a slice of baklava with a Greek coffee to follow. The final indulgence is a small cheroot and a Greek brandy. Then the sun can set.

Long ago, we stumbled on a vegetarian dish known in the Middle East as 'The Prophet fainted' – from pleasure I presume – having consumed this mix of aubergine, onion, tomatoes and cheese, slow baked in the oven. Personally, I had no inclination to faint, no sign of dizziness either, but I will say it is a pretty fine thing when properly made. And the same goes for any and every kind of half decent pizza. Pasta, too, in every form and recipe, with or without beef ragu.

I love fruit, just about any kind. My sister's nickname for me when growing up was 'Apple Boy', so you see I have some cred in this debate. A great lunch that I enjoy is a fruit salad with a buttered bread roll on the side and maybe some blue cheese or French Comte, or a runaway French Brie.

Let's not forget the pulses. Beans are welcome at my table, with or without smoked sausage, pepperoni, or Spanish chorizo. But hold the refried Mexican beans. That is an abomination in my book.

A recipe of my own that is fabulous with fish or chicken is a warm relish that I met in deep southern Languedoc near Cerét, the cherry capital of France, where it was served with fish. When I got home, I tried to recreate it but failed. However, Jan recently bought a bottle of fennel seeds and it all came back to me. Sweat some onions until caramelized, then add chopped ripe tomatoes and a diced red pepper to a pot with a sprinkle of fennel seeds. Simmer till soft and combined. Then add a fresh ripe diced peach or two apricots, or if fresh is not available, use a tinned peach or apricot. Simmer some more and serve with the fish. If you want more anise flavour, add a little Pernod. Serve with the fish in this rough state, or if you want it fancy, then purée the mix in a blender. It's also sublime with grilled prawns, or put the raw prawns into the mix for a minute or two to cook. Served with buttered mashed potato, with the top crisped with more butter and Parmesan. For vegetarians, this relish is so good that it's lovely on its own with the mash.

The case for becoming vegetarian is overwhelming in its arguments. There is no getting away from the fact that eating meat raised industrially is bad for us and for our planet. Why? Greenpeace points out that meat production is the single biggest cause of deforestation globally. In Brazil, farmers deliberately set forest fires in the Amazon to clear the rain forest for cattle ranching and to grow soya for animal feed.

It causes climate change, as meat farming is equivalent to all the driving and flying in the world. And this is pushing the Amazon Forest to a tipping point. Meat production is also responsible for massive human rights abuses and land grabbing from tribes in the Amazon. And it kills wildlife by destroying forests.

Meat eating is an inefficient way to feed the world. Over a quarter of the world's entire land area is used to either graze animals or to grow food for farm animals. If we all ate a plant-based diet, we'd need 75 per cent less farmland than we use today. That is an area of land the equivalent size of the US, China, Europe and Australia combined.

In countries like the UK, we need to eat 70 per cent less meat and dairy by 2030 to prevent climate breakdown. By eating mostly plant-based food, we could feed more people with all the calories and nutrition needed for a healthy diet, without destroying the earth. So enjoy that steak, that lamb cutlet and that pork chop, you may not know it, or want to know it, but it's one of your very last. The Vegetarian Revolution is coming for us all and will do us all good.

CHAPTER 26

PRE-BREAKFAST RIDE

It's the fag end of April 2021 and two weeks after my second Pfizer vaccination, it dawns on me that I've survived the Covid-19 pandemic, despite underlying health issues that has led to many letters and texts from the NHS about shielding. I will be 71 in less than a month. It's a birthday I was not sure I would live to see.

I wake early this morning just before six and hear the wind. It's been the driest April for years and with this persistent cold wind that has blown for weeks and the steady sunshine, the Sussex winter mud is gone. I decide to have a brief early morning ride and then put Callum out to grass for the rest of the day under a New Zealand rug.

We leave the stableyard at eight and drop down the hill behind the cottage to the small stream at the bottom. I give the horse the full length of the reins and he lowers his head to the water and then stops short of it, listening to the sounds of the woods, not wanting to get caught out in this river bottom if dogs come with walkers. His ears flick back and forth and he lifts his head from the water to glance at something off to our right.

He moves off on his own with no urging from me and I take up the slack in the reins. We climb out of the river ravine up towards the Horder Centre, the arthritis clinic, on the next hill and then slant left to follow the stream to another crossing point further west and there he does drink, standing in deeper water. Twenty-two slurps; I count carefully. I'm glad. He is not the greatest water drinker and once had compacted colic as a result. Horses need water to keep the volumes of grass and hay they eat moving along their gut. Once again, he decides when he wants to move on and I let him. He takes such constant direction from me that now and then I let him have a say in the matter and sometimes he surprises me, taking a new path or doubling back even when headed home because he wants to investigate a fallen log or a view, or a break in a holly hedge, or a path he's not been down before.

We lope up the hill to the Church Hill Car Park. These days he no longer goes hell for leather when I give him his head. He's learned to do a lovely Sunday-go-to-church canter, sitting back on his hocks, the most comfortable ground-covering gait a horse can give you. It suits an old man well. I pat his neck in thanks and his ears flick back, acknowledging the touch and the message in it.

He stops on his own before crossing the road. We can't hear any traffic, but he knows that this road is much used by racing cyclists who labour up its steepness or career down it at a blistering pace, which can catch you out with their almost silent approach and speed. But it's clear and we cross.

Now we enter Five Hundred Acre Wood and there is a sparkling of blue and white jewels in the grass-banks, white wood anemones and violets. The beech trees, chestnuts and oaks are all about to leaf and in some places have already. I stop the horse and we take it all in. A new spring. Another one. And not one I was sure I'd make. I take a moment to breathe in deep the forest scents, my lungs unscarred by Covid.

There is a groaning from up the trail and we move on to investigate the sound. It is a plantation of young pines moving in the wind. Some rub on their neighbours making these groaning and creaking noises. Callum is not bothered; he knows this sound and watches the trees make them. A shadow passes over us. It is one of the many buzzards that call this wood home. It is quartering its territory, looking for breakfast. An unwary squirrel, a rabbit, or a pheasant will do nicely. Its whistling cry makes the horse look skyward. He's not a fan of the buzzards, who now and then will buzz us, flying in a low swooping pass just above my head. It makes both me and the horse jump when it happens.

Suddenly I am hungry too and the thought of toast and coffee on the lawn at home makes me urge Callum on. He too will enjoy breakfast on the new protein-rich spring grass in his paddock.

Without my asking, as if reading my mind, he sets off at that lovely slow rolling canter, his 1,600 pounds of muscle and bone – and fighting fit – makes nothing of my 220lbs with tack. Effortlessly, we flow through the white anemone-flaked woods and up the last hill home.

Half an hour later, Callum is in his paddock at the bottom of the hill, right next to his friend Finch. Both have their heads down for some serious sampling of the new grass. I stroll up the hill, take off my chaps and boots, wash my hands and make thick slices of sourdough toast slathered with salted farm butter and the golden-flecked marmalade I am so fond of. I carry it out to my sun-warmed deckchair on the lawn with a steaming mug of filter coffee. Gus comes and lies in my lap, turning his head now and then to check if anything might be coming his way. It's not a bad start to a Sunday. And there are the plentiful remains of a roast leg of lamb in the fridge for lunch, which I will have in a sandwich with raw onion, using the rest in a curry for tonight.

The toast is still warm and the coffee hot. Peace, perfect peace.

CHAPTER 27

GAME FOR THE TABLE

We live on a farm that produces lamb and beef and wild boar for a restaurant in Tunbridge Wells. Well, the boar are not really wild anymore, they are pretty domesticated, which is just as well, because some of them would stand shoulder to shoulder with a Volkswagen Beetle, well almost anyway, and you would not want to tangle with them. And yet Terry, the farm manager, says that on occasion, when they have managed to get out of their enclosure, they have not gone far and have always returned for their supper. Which is most accommodating of them, when you consider that they are going to be someone's supper themselves soon.

You would think that these great beasts of the woods would take off like Sherman tanks for the depths of the forest once they got the merest whiff of freedom. The lure of thousands of acres of forest goodies, acorns, chestnuts, beetles, earthworms, blackberries, mushrooms, the odd sausage dog, would keep them so well fed that their measly enclosure would be the last thought on their minds. But what they think of as a free lunch, provided by kind Terry, holds them hostage. They have not been told that there is no such thing as a free lunch. Greed is not always good, and an easy meal may well be your last if you are a boar.

But it's the truly wild animals that inhabit this place that are on my mind just now. You would not go hungry for a day here in East Sussex if you had a good hunting bow or a rifle. There are herds of deer in the fields and woods all around us, fallow deer mainly but also roe, sika and muntjac. Once you get deep into the forest, you find shooting platforms on some trees that command views across clearings and the length of grassy rides. A handful of people have been given the right to cull the deer. So a little freelance poaching would fill the deep freeze nicely. You would just have to be up to gutting the animal and getting it home, no easy task. But possible to a hungry man or one with a taste for venison. There are flocks of Canada geese that shuttle back and forth at dawn and dusk between ponds and lakes all across the area, and they are semi-tame, so graze at their ease in our horses' paddocks. There is a good spread of rabbits too as the name of our lane attests – Warren Road. There are also the many pheasant that have escaped the shoots in the vicinity and enjoy their freedom, keeping a lookout for foxes, which are their main threat to survival.

The ponds and lakes teem with carp, as the fishermen in their tents on the banks will tell you. If you decided to put sporting chance to one side and simply netted these waters, you would reap enough fish to keep you going for many a day, if you smoked your catch.

But like the boar, we ignore this wild cornucopia and shop at Waitrose or Morrisons or Lidl, law-abiding dutiful drones. God help us if catastrophe cast us back into the wild, we would have to pick up the old hunting skills pretty damn quick or go hungry.

So maybe it's as well to keep one's hand in on how to cook game. The day may come when we will be doing it over campfires and not on gas with cast iron Le Creuset pots. The game is definitely worth the candle. I can remember so well the venison my mother served in Cape Town so many years ago. She would marinade the haunch in red wine, red wine vinegar and bay leaves for a day or two and then stud the meat with chunks of pig fat to add flavour and some fat content to the very lean meat, then, glazed from time to time with an apricot jam mix, the meat would be slowly simmered with wine in a pot-roast. The result was a tender, falling apart flesh that tasted sublime.

Our most common foray into game cooking is with pheasant. This is a bird that lends itself to a variety of cooking methods. You can stuff it and roast it like a chicken but don't overdo it, as its virtually fat free flesh will dry out quickly. We like to pot-roast them in port, and this makes best use of the bird, as every morsel comes off the carcass. With a dash of cream at the end, it is a sufficiently rich dish to satisfy the most demanding gourmand.

Pheasant, wild duck and guinea fowl are all available with venison from your supermarket of choice, but it comes in cellophane and a plastic container without any of the excitement and romance of the chase.

The closest I have ever come to a spot of poaching was to try to bag myself some of the troops of wild guineafowl that roamed Eagle's Nest Estate in Constantia, Cape Town, where I lived many years

ago in my twenties. I tried the old poacher's trick of marinating raisins in brandy and leaving small heaps of them under the trees in which the birds roosted. It was a futile exercise. The birds simply gobbled this alcoholic windfall and flew off. I never got within a stone's throw of any of them and I wasted a perfectly good bottle of KWV brandy. This is a well-named variety, whose nickname in the Cape is 'Koos Wil Vrek' or Koos wants to die. Those guineafowl had patently not heard this expression and were hardened drinkers, it would seem. Getting game for the table is not an easy thing.

See you in the supermarket aisles!

CHAPTER 28

IN PRAISE OF MARMALADE

In the lemon light of an English morning, the orange marmalade glows like a church window with the compressed heat of a Spanish summer. In that jar of jellied fruit live a thousand memories of breakfast-in-bed mornings, of sunlight on a woven cream counterpane, of silence, and the rustle of pages turning; of your sun-kissed skin, your copper hair. It is a fragment of time, bittersweet, like the shards of orange peel encased in amber.

Marmalade, it is an English passion – just how they like it, bottled and kept beneath a lid for safety – a quiet secret indulgence, enjoyed early, with the rest of the day to recover in. It is a passion I share, in this at least we are alike, my no longer new compatriots and me.

There is great pleasure to be had in buying the stuff. It is as various as wine and as the people who make it. There are three-fruit marmalades with lemon, orange and grapefruit, single citrus varieties too, and of course there is the crucialness of cut – the thickness of the peel, coarse medium or fine. There are light and dark, bitter and sweet, and then there are those marmalade masters, the Scots, who add their own passion to the brew to make a heady whisky-mixed concoction for those special occasions. This is a true mix of the heat of the south and that of the north – a melding of hot and cold passions. No wonder I like it.

This strange stuff has evolved and metamorphosed as it moved north. It was named marmalade by the Portuguese who ate a version cooked to the consistency of Turkish delight, thick slabs, golden bricks of it, cut thin and eaten with sharp crumbly white sheep's cheese. But it took the English and Scots to make a sweet jam, as we know it, of this bitter fruit. For the oranges of Seville and Valencia can be sweet or bitter depending on the variety.

Too much can numb the tongue, too little and the craving is not assuaged. Ideally it is served on toast, and must not be drowned in butter, but gild it like lip-gloss on a lovely mouth.

Marmalade has greeted me like an old friend in far-flung places where English is spoken and where it is not. I recall it in the vast echoing dining room of an hotel in the Northern Cape town of Vredendal, where bare-footed waiters padded silently in to bring breakfasts of bacon and eggs to travelling salesmen, comforted in their distance from home by that silver dish of glinting marmalade. Small packs of it have made airline meals and café breakfasts more bearable. I have eaten it above a red tartan carpet in a small inn on the Scottish coast near Oban. I have had it in Israel and Idaho too.

Marmalade is an old, old friend, and one summer I went to its birthplace, to the coast near Valencia. Here the orange trees were planted by those other Africans, the Moors, who would little understand the late arrival of a white African from a place five thousand miles south of them.

They came and conquered as they came, and stayed, and flourished. I came on holiday, a late, a very late, arrival on this much-abused coast, but I too came in search of land, of a place in the sun. But the many cranes, those upside down 'L's' like punctuation marks emphasizing my lateness, swung about their work of building homes for northerners in search of sun. And the orange groves, glinting a hard dark green in the glare gave ground to white villas and concrete blocks, which will also one day distill a bitter sweetness, I suspect, when the new arrivals tire of sun and heat and foreign ways.

And then perhaps the orange trees will once more return and their fruit be shipped north again to people who will eat marmalade and remember their southern escapade as they spoon the sticky shredded jam onto crisp white toast.

We are a secret society, us marmalade eaters, yet the proof of our presence weighs down supermarket shelves everywhere, bulges from displays in speciality food shops and delis. But few know of this passion for the bittersweet, we are protected by the higher profile of the chocoholics and the alcoholics and the biscuit eaters and the doughnut dunkers. Ours is a vice enjoyed in silence at the start of the day, not in smoky nightclubs or in cinema crowds. Our very particular pleasure comes to us when our palates are refreshed and our systems are awake and tingling with that other friend, the steaming coffee cup.

For some there is the passion of night, for others there is afternoon delight and then there's us and our morning madness for marmalade.

CHAPTER 29

FOOD HEROES

If you love food and cooking, you will in time stumble across a new breed – the celebrity chef. Some have been an inspiration to me, even though I've not actually eaten their food, only feasted with my eyes on their TV programmes and picked up some skills, tricks and one or two dishes to replicate as best I can. Two of my food heroes never made it onto the TV screen but both have influenced my cooking. Louis Leipoldt lived and died before the advent of TV in South Africa, and I met him in his books; and another food hero influencer was the diminutive Suzie Meyer, who cooked sublimely for my family for many years.

My first hero is Rick Stein. In my opinion he is the best poet food has ever had. Like me, he struggled at school and it took some years for him to get to university – in his case Oxford, to read English. And boy does it show. He has been touched by tragedy and heartache and this too is evident in the man. To be lost in France, Spain, Portugal, Greece or India with him would be my idea of heaven. His recent offerings of the *Secret France* TV series and his latest series on his beloved Cornwall were meat and drink to me.

I have stood on a Cornish coastal cliff with Rick Stein many and many a time thanks to the magic of television, and listened to him talk, intently, about food, love, life and the universe. For if ever there was a Renaissance man in the kitchen, it's Rick Stein. This gentle, self-deprecating man is a self-taught chef who had his palate educated on trips to France and something of that country's genius fills his work. As does the influence of his second home in Australia.

He is a seemingly very accessible man, open about his history and his past as a one-time nightclub owner and disc jockey in Cornwall and free with insights as to what moves him. References to books, poetry, art and people pepper his conversation. He is interested in others and how they live. And he is amused as he is amusing, and he travels well. His weekends away series gives you wonderful insights into a range of foodie cities across Europe and the world. You come away educated, enriched and hungry for more.

It is not surprising that his love affair with fish and all seafood has led him to own several fish restaurants in Padstow in Cornwall and elsewhere. I believe there are very long waits to get a booking for a table in any of them. He is unique among chefs for bringing fish to our tables in such quantity, something the island-bound British are lukewarm about unless it is served wrapped in batter with chips from the local fish and chip shop. Fish is Rick's passion.

As a fisherman myself, there is no greater pleasure than accompanying Rick out onto a Cornish bay in some old fishing boat with a local fisherman as a guide, bringing in lobster or crab pots or fishing for mackerel and then returning home to Rick's kitchen to see what he does with it. He is an astonishingly good ambassador for food and the pleasures of the table. Personally, I think he is a national treasure, just like the poet John Betjeman who lies in the small graveyard of St Enodoc's Church at Trebetherick, just across the Camel River estuary from Rick Stein's Padstow. John Betjeman's obituarist in *The Times* thought the poet 'a true original', and considered that he was 'whimsical, imprudent, shrewd, humorous, disarming.' The same can be said of Rick Stein, and the man also cooks like a dream.

His signature dish, or one that lingers in the mind, is perhaps that fantastic annual fish barbecue on the beach that he produces for his restaurant staff, or maybe a shellfish risotto, or perhaps a perfectly grilled sea bass. When I see that there is a new Rick Stein TV series coming my way, I am filled with joy at the prospect of watching him once more. Though I wish he'd get a dog again. I do miss Chalky, his longhaired Jack Russell who died some years back, and Rick's interaction with him.

Then there is the wild-haired, bespectacled, punning chef, Hugh Fearnley-Whittingstall, another favourite of mine. He is based down at River Cottage in Dorset and is perhaps best known for his commitment to seasonal, ethically produced food and his concern for the environment. His TV programmes give muscle to the idea of self-sufficiency, of living off the land, raising your own chickens, pigs, lamb and also scouring the local countryside and the nearby coast and sea for edible ingredients. In a way he exemplifies the back to the soil movement.

He is a great food educator, introducing us to foods we might not have thought to try, and some which he gives a radical new twist to, then going into food markets to road-test his new recipes. He has earned a huge following through his *River Cottage* TV series and books, as well as campaigns such as Hugh's Fish Fight, Hugh's War on Waste and his latest, Britain's Fat Fight.

There is something gentle yet uncompromising about him and he seems unafraid to be his own slightly eccentric self. He makes for very good company on the box. There is a puckish humour to his broadcast work and I for one would not be surprised to find him living in an oak tree, whipping up delicious dishes for the animal denizens of the woods. He is an original and someone to be grateful for. His advocacy for wild foods and foraging brings with it a love and respect for Mother Nature and gels with my own interest in animism and the genius of place, *genius loci,* that I have tried to explore in my own writing.

His signature dishes might include something vegetarian like his roast root hummus, or a perfectly roasted farmyard chicken for Sunday lunch, or maybe a belly of pork Chinese style from his own porkers.

Marco Pierre White was the youngest chef in his time to get three Michelin stars and then gave them away after some time, saying 'been there, done that'. In his heyday, he apparently took no hostages and did not suffer fools in any way. If he appears to be a somewhat brusque man, so be it, but he is one who cooks like a dream. Marco gets a bad rap as an enfant terrible, as someone who does not hesitate to vent anger. I don't know him, have never met him, nor eaten at any of his restaurants, but a man who cooks like him, who rose to the top with a fierce and focused attention, who showed Britain what the best looked like and tasted like, and took pride in delivering the best, is worthy of respect in my book. And his relinquishing his awards to follow another path speaks to me of something in his make-up worthy of even greater respect. He intrigues me.

As a signature dish? I hope he does not think me presumptuous in selecting one of his dishes that I would love to try – sea bass stuffed with a mousse of scallops is the one I would choose to linger over.

Jamie Oliver, the charming dyslexic genius who brought real food to a huge new audience in Britain, making it accessible and understandable and changing what our schools served their pupils is another of my heroes. Wearing his heart on his sleeve, Jamie is a true revolutionary. This cheeky chappie managed to lobby the government in the UK to do something about food in schools and this may be his longest and single greatest legacy. He tossed turkey twizzlers out of school kitchens and gave us the greatest steak sandwich among his many signature dishes.

Not surprisingly, he is a fantastically effective communicator, making the preparation of food look easy and appetizing. He is the sort of chap it would be good to have along, if ever you were stranded on a desert island. He has been an inspiration to a whole generation of young chefs to whom he gave a start in one of his many restaurant kitchens.

To be with him through his TV series, in his camper van on a tour of Italy, shopping in local markets and cooking in vineyards or by the sea, was a great pleasure. The way he interacts with an Italian grandma in her own kitchen and the delight he inspires in a Palermo food market is a joy to watch. Jamie speaks that truly international language, simpatico, and the language of food.

The irascible chef, Keith Floyd (1943-2009), was an English celebrity cook, restaurateur, TV personality and 'gastronaut', who brought a panache and style to cooking on TV that was uniquely his own.

On television, his style of presentation was eccentric; his habit of drinking copious amounts of wine as he cooked while scolding his crew endeared him to millions of viewers worldwide. He made it real and he made it glamorous at the same time. And he made me smile and on occasion laugh out loud with some madcap behaviour or comment.

With Keith Floyd, there was no bullshit, just a great deal of temperament and personality, but I would hasten to accept any invitation he offered to eat at his table. You would know that you were about to have the meal of a lifetime.

If you have to find a signature dish for Keith Floyd you could do worse than settling on pan-fried chicken stuffed with cheese and pistachio nuts, or beef in tomato sauce with green olives, perhaps coconut-curried fish. I hesitate to settle on anything really, in case his short-tempered spirit decides to visit me one night for having the nerve to speak for him.

The loss of Anthony Bourdain is still felt around the world by many who admired him and who loved his TV work. I was among those who felt pained by his untimely death at his own hand. This tall, gangly, intrepid traveller, cook and substance abuser, was simply the coolest dude since Steve McQueen. Every man wanted to be him, every woman just wanted him. Dead at the pinnacle of his fame, his appetite for life is writ large across all his film work for TV.

He was fearless and would eat just about anything in the many exotic or remote places he filmed in. He would put things in his mouth directly from kitchen fires or chemical laboratories that most of us would gag on. He went where no chef has been before and he made it fun. His signature dish? Only God knows; where do I start? The man loved burgers and barbecue and hot dogs as well as haute cuisine. Let's settle on a Portuguese fish stew, something I would be happy to share with him. But the crab claws are mine, Tony!

His books include *Kitchen Confidential* and *Medium Raw* among many others. Get them, you are in for a wild ride and a great treat. The man was a rock star.

Suzy Meyer, my family's cook for thirty years is a food hero of mine, the first in fact. Less than five foot tall, this tiny woman cooked like a dream, day in and day out, three meals a day for a family of five plus five servants, with a choice of main courses and desserts. I do not know how she did it without complaint, with great good humour and with consistent excellence. Her food was outstanding.

It shames me now to think that I would tease her about her love life, which to the best of my knowledge was as blameless as that of a nun. She was wedded to that damn stove at our home in the Cape. I think she was profoundly shy and self-contained. She said very little but that with good humour, always. I was very fond of her.

She produced great soups, wonderful meat roasts, stews, and fish dishes. She made great curries and desserts to die for. And God bless her, she cooked those damn wind-dried mullet – *bokkoms* – so beloved by my father, that stank the kitchen out. And she made brawn and tripe for my parents that nobody else would touch. She had a huge repertoire. One of my favourite meals of hers would have to be beef stroganoff, followed by one of her trifles, maybe a lemon meringue tart or a slice of her cherry-topped, three-inch tall cheesecake, or best of all and my favourite, *appeliepie tert*, a golden puff pastry tart topped with great golden Cape gooseberries.

Wherever you are now, Suzy, I wish you well and thank you for putting up with my teenage nonsense. Your great food fed my stomach and my soul, and your menus informed my food education and now these words that I write. *Dankie!*

Louis Leipoldt (1880-1947) was a South African poet, playwright, paediatrician, botanist, journalist, novelist, cook and a connoisseur of food and wine. His life intrigues me. Because his mother insisted that he be home schooled, he learned about the preparation of food from the family cook Maria, while also learning to speak fluent English, German, Dutch, Latin and Greek. Maria taught him her skills in preparing slow cooked stews or *bredies,* as well as her knowledge of herbs and plant medicine.

His books include *Kos vir die Kenner* (Food for the

Connoisseur) and his *Cape Cookery* is a classic. His work is filled with exotic indigenous dishes from supreme of flamingo to tortoise stew. As someone who has actually cooked a tortoise, all I can say is that he must have been a better cook than me to get anyone to eat tortoise. The major part of my tortoise, found and cooked while on South African Army manoeuvres, stayed in the fire.

His grave lies in a romantic cave in the Cedarberg near Clanwilliam in the Cape, which still bears the signs of San Bushmen rock painting. He was a great soul, with an encyclopaedic knowledge of many subjects, and an inspired cook to boot.

And as a signature dish, I'd like to try his tortoise. Oh yes. Anthony Bourdain I'm eating this in memory of you. God keep you all a place at his table.

What have I learned from my heroes if anything, other than the knowledge that I will never be their equal in the kitchen? I suppose three or four things: buy local; buy the best ingredients you can afford; and don't mess with it too much, keep it simple. If there is a fourth it would be to never stop experimenting and trying new things. I know there are fruits and vegetables out there that I have yet to taste. As and when I do, I will refer to these heroes to see what they made of this new stuff and so deepen my knowledge and my pleasure. And finally, and crucially, bring a good appetite to the meal; hunger is indeed the best sauce.

CHAPTER 30

CUPBOARD LOVE

We pretend to love shopping but it's a chore at the best of times. Does anyone enjoy shopping in supermarkets? I for one don't. I dislike the aggro in the car park, the numbers of other shoppers, the vast offering on display – consumerism taken to the nth degree. The whole business of queuing to unload the trolley and pack as fast as you can into bags that I for one forget from time to time and am forced to pay for more plastic bags. But I must admit it is convenient. And one does make some unexpected discoveries. The Covid-19 pandemic, however, has shown us how to save time and money by staying out of supermarkets. Some of us won't be returning, I suspect. The home delivery drivers and their back-up packers are among the heroes of this past year, helping to keep the old and the clinically vulnerable safe and fed at home.

Yet, strangely enough, I think that for older customers the supermarket offers a benefit other than simply shopping for food, it's an opportunity to socialise, bump into friends and maybe grab a coffee and a Danish. For many it offers a neutral space where little is expected of you and others are available, not behind laptops or on phones. And for this, if nothing else, I believe supermarkets offer a useful service at a time when loneliness is a pandemic all of its own, with more people than ever living on their own and isolated from others.

But the whole raison d'être of supermarkets is to tempt you to spend more. And in its way, that is an education. Think of the foreign foods now freely available either ready cooked and chilled or the ingredients to make your own. Italian, Indian, Chinese, Thai meals, are all there. It's a gustatory world tour.

My own personal experience of supermarkets includes seven years of behind-the-scenes contact with supermarket chains in South Africa. But the principles observed there are universal. As a biscuit salesman for my father's bakery in Cape Town, I was a regular visitor to the headquarters of Pick 'n Pay, one of the country's leading chains. It was not a visit I ever looked forward to. The food buyer I dealt with had just one object in mind, to beat down the price using every method he could, including the threat of removing our brand from their shelves. He would denigrate the product and be personally offensive. It was standard procedure for dealing with all suppliers. Young and naïve as I was, it shocked me, seeing at first-hand how capitalism worked, up close and personal.

Besides my brief, which was to sell biscuits, I also got involved in promotions and merchandising, which meant fighting for space on the supermarket shelves and against the encroachment by the salesmen and merchandisers of other rival brands. It was ruthless. An allocation of a gondola end – the front-facing shelves near the checkouts – was a major victory and another six inches in the biscuit shelves another triumph.

I got to know the individual managers who were in jobs that were high stress. They had to cope with targets set by headquarters, the clamouring of salesmen at their open public desks on the supermarket floor, and the complaints of their customers, sometimes loud and offensive. It was not a job for the faint of heart.

The warehouses behind the shop itself or upstairs, where thousands of boxes of stock were stacked, metres high, were usually a cool, relatively quiet escape from the tensions on the floor of the shop. Here I would take stock of what we had on the premises and take down boxes for pricing and display on the supermarket shelves. Now and then I would chance on a couple of workers kissing and cuddling beneath the cardboard towers.

So today, when I walk into a supermarket, this personal history colours my experience. I see beyond the scenes of brightly stacked fruit and veg, beyond the biscuit and confectionery aisles to the quiet depths of the warehouse behind, or above, and the human interactions from farmers to transporters, to stacking staff who brought all of this product to these square metres of space. It is an immense undertaking and a triumph in many ways, but it is not always in our best interest. The quality of the food, the price and the ethical methods used in its production is questionable at times and on occasion despicable. But it's the best system we have, for now.

Keeping those shelves stocked is a 24-hour operation seven days a week and involves armies of warehouse staff, transport drivers and shelf stackers working around the clock.

Sometimes size is not everything and I love stocking up in the local farm shops in East Sussex where you will find organic fruit and vegetables produced on the spot, hand reared meat and the produce of small specialist bakers, as well as a few women who have perfected the art of cake baking, jam making, or the production of chutneys and relishes. Local cheeses are also available. These places are gems and we should support them in their battle to survive the onslaught of the supermarkets. One of the things about them I particularly like is the staff who quite often seem to be the last of the hippies and I suspect come from California in Sussex, as Forest Row is known, with its alternative education infrastructure and earth- loving locals.

I may be somewhat biased but the best farm shops I've encountered are those in the Cape, land of my birth. On the drive over Sir Lowry's Pass and Du Toit Kloof Pass there are a sprinkling of these establishments, which stock an array of mouth-watering treats: home-baked bread and cake; biscuits and my beloved buttermilk rusks; koeksisters; milk tarts; meebos; dried fruits; olives; a dazzling choice of pies; a dozen or more flavours of biltong and dried sausage; boerewors; and the ripest most flavourful fruit I have ever tasted outside of a French market. There are jams and chutneys, jars of green figs in syrup, and walls stacked with wine from every vineyard for fifty miles around. You can run amok in these places, if you are of the foodie persuasion, and on occasion I have.

Then by way of comparison, there is food shopping in the rawest, most direct way imaginable. Come with me to Kalk Bay (Chalk Bay) on the False Bay coast of the Cape Peninsula in South Africa, where the mountains rise almost from the shore and where you will find a rough fishing harbour, home to a fleet of little fishing trawlers and a handful of larger vessels that work this part of the coast for its huge bounty. The crews are from the local Coloured fishing community that has been here for generations. They lose boats and friends to the sea regularly, for this is not a gentle sea. Here the two currents that follow the African coast meet briefly and split. The warm Agulhas Current tears up the east coast at speeds of five knots and more and the cold Benguela heads north up the west coast. When tides, wind and current are at cross-purposes, these two coastlines eat men and ships with a ferocious appetite. Despite this, the fishermen of Kalk Bay go to sea year round and reap a harvest of outstanding fish varieties that in my opinion is the best in the world. They bring in tuna, yellow tail, kabeljou, hake, kingklip and snoek, among others too numerous to mention.

If you love fish as I do, then a visit to the Kalk Bay quays when the boats come in is a must. Teams of women gut and clean the cascades of great silver fish for you in the sheds on the quayside. I love it all, but if I had to choose a favourite it would have to be the fighting yellowtail whose firm white meaty flesh is incomparable. The flakier kabeljou is also exceptional and the oily snoek either grilled fresh or, better yet, barbecued with a slather of apricot jam, makes for a feast. You can smoke it too and when still warm served with Cape gooseberry jam and buttered fresh warm bread, it is a meal fit for the gods. It is also fabulous turned into a mousse to spread on toast.

This is shopping as sport. You have to be quick and have your wits about you and you'd best be prepared for some salty language and jokes at your expense; these fishwives take no prisoners. I've been in many a fish market in Europe and they are justly famed for their offerings, but for the sheer fun of the thing and for the quality on sale, give me Kalk Bay every time.

Another opportunity to shop at the edge of the sea was something I had the privilege to observe throughout my childhood on the beaches at Bloubergstrand, near Cape Town, where we had a holiday home. Coloured fishermen kept wooden dories drawn up on the dunes at the top of these beaches and in season would keep watch for the arrival of shoals of harders, a South African mullet known to scientists as *Chelon richardsonii.* When the call came, the boats loaded with nets would be rushed down the beach and into the surf. A crew of four or six men would take up the oars and row like demons to get through the breaking waves. One end of the net would be held by one or more men on the beach. After a rapid row in a half-moon curve, the boat would surf in through the breakers a hundred yards further up the beach. Now the fishermen would be joined by onlookers to haul in the net and in some fifteen or twenty minutes a mass of hundreds, sometimes thousands of thrashing silver harders, around a foot long, would be dragged up the beach and transferred into wicker baskets. At this point, money would change hands for six or a dozen fish and supper would have been secured. Our family ate them regularly throughout their brief season, grilled, or fried. When salted and wind-dried, they are known as bokkoms, and my father loved these as a snack with drinks or as a starter.

There is much of the old hunter-gatherer still in our make-up as a species and foraging for your own food, whether in the woods or in the sea, brings with it a tang of pleasure like no other. When our children were young, we would collect chestnuts in the woods in Sussex and fill punnets with the huge crop of blackberries in the hedgerows around the cottage, turning them into pies or simply serving them with sugar and cream.

It is not surprising that so many people still prefer the pleasure of shopping in food markets, as in France, where the farmers who produced the food on their land stand before you to sell it. This system ensures that by and large what you are getting is local, fresh and in season. And you can quiz the grower on his or her methods of production. This is not a place offering strawberries in December, flown in from Kenya. And there is no middleman demanding rock-bottom prices to put the food before you or insisting on the shape of the produce. Personally, I love markets. No holiday is complete without multiple visits, if possible, to shop daily for our food. It is a pleasure and a joy. And the subsequent pleasure of cooking is enhanced, as is the eating of the end product.

At the last French market we visited in La Rochelle, we were blown away by the quality and variety of the produce, some of which we had never come across before. The different kinds of tomatoes never fail to amaze me, the scent and colour of the strawberries, apricots and peaches dazzle. The cheese, the fish, the meat, the charcuterie, the flan makers, the stall with its freight of huge golden gleaming chickens turning on spits, the offering seems endless, and as I meander through, tasting this and sampling that, ideas and images and recipes pass through my mind. It is utterly compelling and entrancing to a committed foodie. There is nothing like it. The experience is the very opposite of supermarket shopping.

And you simply have to ask for help or advice to be deluged with assistance from the stall holders and fellow shoppers, each one offering you their favourite way of preparing and serving the prawns you are buying or the huge asparagus. Humour is ever present in this setting, from the joshing between stallholders to the little-understood sallies between customer and stallholder, but the vitality and amusement is there for all to see.

You are involved in a human activity almost as old as man, the provisioning of your larder from the communal market. The experience teaches you not only about food, but about the people who bring it to you and the area you live in. It is a lesson in maths, botany, geography, history and psychology all rolled into one. It is food shopping as theatre and entertainment and speaking personally, I find it hard to drag myself away from it, fearful that I might just have missed that artisan cheese or that new variety of green beans or the woman who churns her own butter and stamps it with an embossed cow image and wraps it in straw. Who can resist this stuff? I can't. And as a result, we eat better.

I cannot write about food shopping without once more mentioning a crucial, memorable, never-to-be-forgotten, life-changing food shopping experience. We walked into a delicatessen in Paris for the first time and I was overwhelmed by the sights and smells and the variety on offer, the pre-prepared meals to take away including butter- and cheese-topped scallops, veal in a variety of sauces, chicken casseroles, ratatouille and endless salamis and cheeses and hams. I must have looked shellshocked and dazed, because the shop owner came up to me, put his hand on my shoulder and said: *'Courage, mon brave. Courage!'* He was being funny, but in his comment too there was an acknowledgement that I was dazzled by the best of France, and he was justly proud of it.

In my food shopping experience, that delicatessen colours my search for shops that reach that standard, that when you see it, something profound about the culture you are in stands revealed, self-evidently. And you are instantly enriched by the experience. Shopping for food with passion can be a rewarding and fulfilling experience for more than just your stomach.

CHAPTER 31

MAKING A MEAL OF IT

It's one thing to write about food in an idealistic, enthusiastic or romantic way, but what I actually consume sometimes gives me pause. My diet is heavy on bread, meat and salt, which I know only too well is not good for me. Chocolate and biscuits feature too. But change does not seem to be coming any time soon. I suppose my saving grace is that I eat lots of fruit and veg and cook with olive oil and drink very modestly. And my horse keeps me fit with mucking out, grooming, exercising and walking him to and from his paddock each day.

Reading previous chapters, it sounds as though each meal is something special or rare and exotic. The truth is much more mundane. Our everyday menu is simpler altogether. That is not to say we don't occasionally cook up a storm or eat out and enjoy something delicious, but our day-to-day breakfast, lunch and supper would not be worthy of a great cookbook.

I take courage from watching the late chef Anthony Bourdain sit down after a long day of eating, cooking and filming with a hotdog or a hamburger and a beer. And he looks particularly happy then. Few people, even the very top chefs, can manage exotic grub constantly. In every life, pizza, pasta, burgers and chips must be on the menu occasionally.

Breakfast is easy, invariably toast and marmalade with my second coffee of the day. In summer, Greek yogurt with fruit honey and nuts. In winter I will have porridge from time to time.

Lunch is usually a sandwich of some kind, tuna, or bacon, or cheese and tomato and a piece of fruit and a coffee. Sometimes leftovers from the night before and in winter a bowl of soup and a bread roll.

Supper is our big meal of the day – against all the advice of medics and that expression – breakfast like a king, lunch like a prince, dine like a pauper. In fact, dinner is usually a piece of meat – chicken, chops, steak, sausage with vegetables, or a stew and occasionally fish, and if so, it is usually salmon or cod, followed up invariably in my case with a slice of toast and jam and my last mug of coffee for the day. Coffee has no effect on my ability to sleep.

Jan and I sort out our own breakfast and lunch and take turns cooking supper. I am blessed in having Jan to cook for and sitting opposite me for dinner as she is a good cook herself but will be happy with whatever I serve, be it a baked potato with cheese and salad or a full-on production.

There is something about cooking that I find deeply calming and satisfying and although the results are not always to my satisfaction, now and then I get it right and this gives me real pleasure. I just wish that BBC Radio 4 would axe its 6.30 to 7pm slot, filled with light comedy, and give us something more interesting to cook by. Imagine having *The History of the World in a Hundred Objects* with former Director of the British Museum, Neil MacGregor, retelling humanity's history through the objects we have made. I'm sure my cooking would improve.

Currently the news programmes are filled with a story about our comic opera villain Prime Minister, Boris Johnson, whose refurbishment of Number 10 Downing Street and the hullaballoo about who paid for it, the £56,000 used to upgrade the kitchen and to provide new curtains and cushions. Like the rest of the country, I shake my head at this latest evidence of political sleaze. Our own kitchen is some thirty years old and doing just fine. I like the mix of russet clay floor tiles and pale oak cabinets with mismatched china doorknobs in cream and blue, matching the tiles above the hob with their ceramic reliefs of foxes and hares. It has served us well and we eat supper in the kitchen each evening, looking up the garden to the woods beyond. Our hob needs replacing, as currently just two of the gas rings function properly, and in time we will get round to it.

Our kitchen implements are the usual mix and the pots and pans all hardy survivors with one or two newer arrivals. Central to our cooking implements are two vintage Le Creuset casserole pots, the larger one red, the smaller blue. If they could speak no doubt they would talk of the chicken, lamb and beef stews, the curries and the casseroles they have produced over the years. They owe us little and continue to provide excellent service. I see them as old friends and we are thinking of giving a new big one to Dom and Steph as a house-warming gift.

The process of deciding what to have for supper starts, if it's my turn to cook, with a selection first thing in the morning, usually from our deep freeze in the utility room; some chicken, or lamb chops, steak or sausage is the usual fare. Now and then duck breasts, or beef mince for a bolognaise ragu. It will defrost in the fridge all day, ready for cooking at 6pm for supper at 7pm. The deep freeze, dare I say it, also contains, bread and milk, and steak pies, fish pies, and chicken and leek pies for those times when cooking is just too much of a chore.

But I like the gentle rhythm of this food preparation whatever else is going on in our lives. Come 6pm and I will have a bag of salt and vinegar crisps with a drink, usually a G&T, and start the process of preparing supper.

Our weekend routine is much the same but when summer finally arrives in East Sussex we move outdoors as much as we can. This means barbecues and meals taken outside on our old wobbly teak table and benches under the rowan tree. Given half a chance Gus, our rescue dog – half King Charles, half Pomeranian – will scoot up off the grass to sit alongside us on the bench and keep a sharp eye on the movement of food on the table from platters to plates to mouths. Invariably his patience is rewarded, and he skips ahead of us when we carry the plates back to the kitchen, looking back over his shoulder, hoping for more. He is the ultimate optimist.

In a world that has taken to buying pre-cooked meals and having hot food delivered to our doors, there is a danger that our children will forget how to cook altogether, and what a pleasure they will be denying themselves. You could make a case that we are the 'Cooking Animal', the only one on earth to cook its food before consuming it.

So we need to teach our kids about the joy of food shopping, food preparation and cooking, because in time they may well be cooking for us at the end. Imagine ending your days waiting for a tikka masala from Deliveroo? God save us all from that fate, an empty fridge, a dusty larder with a few out-of-date tins. The thought of food cooked miles away, possibly in another country, arriving with the ringing of the front door bell. The thought makes my blood run cold.

Julian Roup
East Sussex
October, 2021

Other titles by the authors for your consideration:

No Faff, No Fuss, Just Food
By Maryanne Coleman

No Fuss, No Faff, Just Food is a cookery book for people who have better things to do than slave over a hot stove. Filled with suggestions as well as recipes and thoughtfully peppered with pages for your own ideas, this book takes the lid off the simmering worries which many people have when cooking for themselves, family and friends – cooking should be fun, not scary, and reading this romp through possibly the most relaxed kitchen in the world will have you laughing as well as, very soon, cooking like you mean it!

Recipes in *No Fuss, No Faff, Just Food* include main meals, snacks, basic techniques and – of course – chocolate cake! There's no point in a recipe book with no chocolate cake in it and as a bonus, it is gluten and dairy free! Safety in the kitchen, from sharp knives to anaphylactic shock, avoidance of, is covered as well as some yummy recipes.

If you only ever have one cookery book, make it this one.

The Children's Crusade
By M. J. Trow

In the summer of 1212, 30,000 children from towns and villages all over France and Germany left their homes and families and began a crusade. Their aim; to retake Jerusalem, the holiest city in the world, for God and for Christ. They carried crosses and they believed, because the Bible told them so, that they could cross the sea like Moses. The walls of Jerusalem would fall, like Jericho's did for Joshua.

It was the age of miracles – anything was possible. Kings ignored the Children; so did popes and bishops. The handful of Church chroniclers who wrote about them were usually disparaging. They were delusional, they were inspired not by God, but the Devil. Their crusade was doomed from the start.

None of them reached Outremer, the Holy Land. They turned back, exhausted. Some fell ill on the way; others died. Others still were probably sold into slavery to the Saracens – the very Muslims who had taken Jerusalem in the first place.

We only know of three of them by name – Stephen, Nicholas and Otto. One of them was a shepherd, another a ploughboy, the third a scholar. The oldest was probably fourteen. Today, in a world where nobody believes in miracles, the Children of 1212 have almost been forgotten.

Almost… but not quite…

The poet Robert Browning caught the mood in his haunting poem, *The Pied Piper of Hamelin*, bringing to later readers the sad image of a lost generation, wandering a road to who knew where.

Consumed
By Justin Alcala

Sergeant Nathaniel Brannick is trapped in Victorian London during a period of disease, crime, and insatiable vices. One night, Brannick returns from work to find an eerie messenger in his flat who warns him of dark things to come.

When his next case involves a victim who suffered from consumption, he uncovers clues that lead him to believe the messenger's warning. Despite his incredulity, he can't help but wonder if the practical man he once was has been altered by an investigation encompassed in the paranormal. That is, until he meets the witch hunters, and everything takes a turn for the worse.

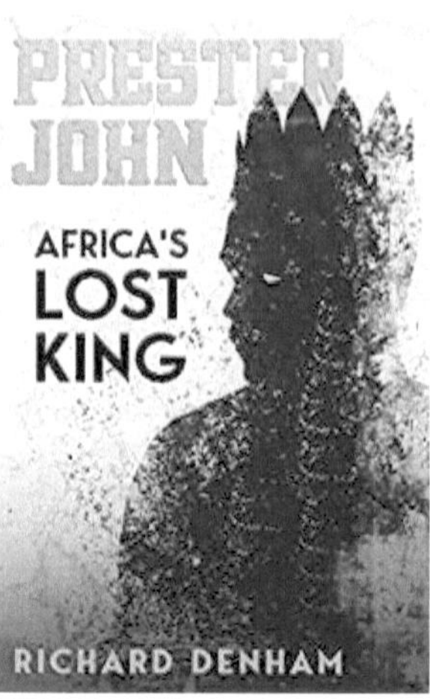

Prester John: Africa's Lost King
By Richard Denham

He sits on his jewelled throne on the Horn of Africa in the maps of the sixteenth century. He can see his whole empire reflected in a mirror outside his palace. He carries three crosses into battle and each cross is guarded by one hundred thousand men. He was with St Thomas in the third century when he set up a Christian church in India. He came like a thunderbolt out of the far East eight centuries later, to rescue the crusaders clinging on to Jerusalem. And he was still there when Portuguese explorers went looking for him in the fifteenth century.

He went by different names. The priest who was also a king was Ong Khan; he was Genghis Khan; he was Lebna Dengel. Above all, he was a Christian king who ruled a vast empire full of magical wonders: men with faces in their chests; men with huge, backward-facing feet; rivers and seas made of sand.

Was he real? Did he ever exist? This book will take you on a journey of a lifetime, to worlds that might have been, but never were. It will take you, if you are brave enough, into the world of Prester John.

Goblin Market
By Maryanne Coleman

Have you ever wondered what happened to the faeries you used to believe in? They lived at the bottom of the garden and left rings in the grass and sparkling glamour in the air to remind you where they were. But that was then – now you might find them in places you might not think to look. They might be stacking shelves, delivering milk or weighing babies at the clinic. Open your eyes and keep your wits about you and you might see them.

But no one is looking any more and that is hard for a Faerie Queen to bear and Titania has had enough. When Titania stamps her foot, everyone in Faerieland jumps; publicity is what they need. Television, magazines. But that sort of thing is much more the remit of the bad boys of the Unseelie Court, the ones who weave a new kind of magic; the World Wide Web.

Here is Puck re-learning how to fly; Leanne the agent who really is a vampire; Oberon's Boys playing cards behind the wainscoting; Black Annis, the bag-lady from Hainault, all gathered in a Restoration comedy that is strictly twenty-first century.

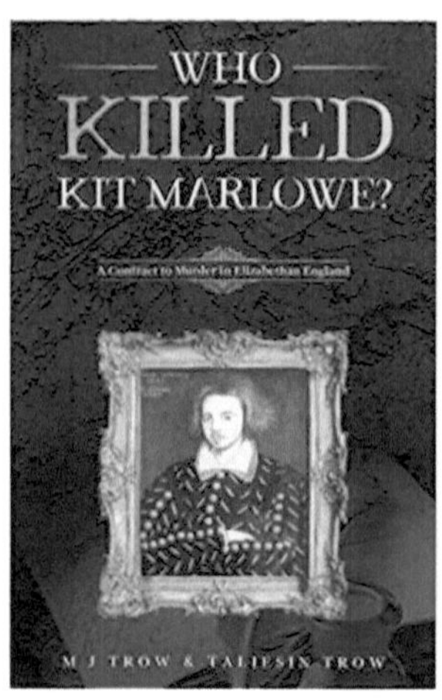

Who Killed Kit Marlowe?: A Contract to Murder in Elizabethan England
By M. J. Trow & Taliesin Trow

Kit Marlowe was the bad boy of Elizabethan drama. His 'mighty line' of iambic pentameter transformed the miracle plays of the Middle Ages into modern drama and he paved the way for Shakespeare and a dozen other greats who stole his metre and his ideas. When he died, stabbed through the eye in what appeared to be a tavern brawl in Deptford in May 1593, he was only 29 and many people believed that he had met his just deserts.

But Marlowe's death was not the result of a brawl. And it did not take place in a tavern. The facts tell a different story, one involving intrigue, espionage, alchemy and the highest in the land.

The brutal murder of a young playwright at the peak of his powers has intrigued and captivated for over 400 years. This compelling journey through the evidence allows us to know, for the first time, who killed him.

Fade
By Bethan White

Do you want to remember?

Do you want to forget?

There is nothing extraordinary about Chris Rowan. Each day he wakes to the same faces, has the same breakfast, the same commute, the same sort of homes he tries to rent out to unsuspecting tenants.

There is nothing extraordinary about Chris Rowan. That is apart from the black dog that haunts his nightmares and an unexpected encounter with a long forgotten demon from his past. A nudge that will send Chris on his own downward spiral, from which there may be no escape.

There is nothing extraordinary about Chris Rowan...

www.blkdogpublishing.com

www.ingramcontent.com/pod-product-compliance
Ingram Content Group UK Ltd.
Pitfield, Milton Keynes, MK11 3LW, UK
UKHW040006200726
13854UKWH00001B/74